WORLD RESOURCES INSTITUTE

THE "SECOND INDIA" REVISITED:

Population, Poverty, and Environmental Stress over Two Decades

ROBERT REPETTO

THE "SECOND INDIA" REVISITED:
Population, Poverty, and Environmental Stress
Over Two Decades

Robert Repetto

WORLD RESOURCES INSTITUTE

August 1994

Kathleen Courrier
Publications Director

Brooks Belford
Marketing Manager

Hyacinth Billings
Production Manager

Mark Edwards/Earthscan
Cover Photo

Each World Resources Institute Report represents a timely, scholarly treatment of a subject of public concern. WRI takes responsibility for choosing the study topics and guaranteeing its authors and researchers freedom of inquiry. It also solicits and responds to the guidance of advisory panels and expert reviewers. Unless otherwise stated, however, all the interpretation and findings set forth in WRI publications are those of the authors.

Contents

Acknowledgments v

Foreword vii

Collaborators ix

I. Overview 1
    A. Background to the Study 1
    B. The Main Trends 4
    C. Vicious and Virtuous Circles 6
    D. The Primacy of Institutions and of
       Policies 8

II. Population Change in India: A 20-Year
     Perspective 11
     A. Changing Mortality Patterns 11
     B. Falling Birth Rates 13
     C. India's Family Planning Programs . . . 15
     D. Social and Cultural Determinants of
        Demographic Change 16

III. Macroeconomic Developments,
     Employment, and Poverty 21
     A. Growth and Structural Change 21
     B. Labor Force, Employment and
        Wages 23
     C. Poverty Trends 26
     D. Reasons Behind the Growth
        Acceleration 27

IV. Food, Agriculture, and Water 31
    A. Change in Nutritional Status 33
    B. Agricultural Production 35
    C. Agricultural Land Scarcity 37
    D. Increasing Use of Chemicals 38
    E. Expansion in Tubewell Irrigation 41
    F. Continuing Problems with Canal
       Irrigation 43

G. Rural Employment 45
H. Agricultural Price Policies 46

V. India's Rural Off-Farm Environment 49
    A. Importance of Common Property
       Resources 49
    B. Shrinking Common Property
       Resources and the Economic
       Effects 50
    C. Effects on Rural Poverty 53
    D. Effects on Biodiversity 54

VI. Urbanization, Urban Poverty, and the
     Urban Environment 57
     A. Urbanization Patterns 57
     B. Urban Poverty 58
     C. Environmental Hazards and Effects
        on Health 59

VII. Energy, Population, and the
     Environment 65
     A. The *Second India Study's*
        Assessment 65
     B. Actual Rural Energy Developments . . 68
     C. Petroleum Demand and Supply 70
     D. Electric Power 72

VIII. Industry 77
      A. Indian Industrial Policy at the Time
         of the *Second India Study* 77
      B. The *Second India Study's* Alternative
         Vision and its Fate 79
      C. Industry's Environmental Impacts . . . 80
      D. Accelerated Growth in the 1980s 84

IX. Facing the Future 87

X.   References 91

Acknowledgments

*T*he *"Second India" Revisited* is the fruit of a truly collaborative research effort.

Although the World Resources Institute contributed the initial impetus to undertake the study and assembled the study team, the participants listed on Page ix made the major contribution in defining the issues and bringing to bear a wealth of information, research experience, and seasoned judgment in their fields of expertise. By mutual agreement, this report's author had the limited role of condensing the more extensive papers contributed by all collaborators and synthesizing them into an integrated report. By far the largest share of information and conclusions in this report is that of the collaborators. The author has made use of material from other sources mostly to fill gaps and to shed light on topics not fully covered in collaborators' contributions. Nonetheless, synthesizing and generalizing from this wealth of material inevitably involves making judgments, and for these the author takes responsibility. Although the contributors have thoroughly reviewed and commented on drafts of this report, not all collaborators would necessarily agree with all that it contains. It deals with complicated issues. Indian scholars do not always agree with each other on these issues; there is no reason why they should all agree with me.

In addition to the listed collaborators, to whom I am deeply grateful for their many contributions, thanks are due to other participating scholars: Veena Joshi, Dean of the Policy Analysis Group at the Tata Energy Research Institute, S.C. Gulati from the Institute of Economic Growth, and B. Venkata Rao from the Administrative Staff College of India. I also thank John Cool and Hannan Ezekiel, instrumental figures in the original *Second India Study*, for their information and counsel. Anukriti Sud, Alec Koch, and Carrie Meyer have assisted and participated in the project at WRI. I also wish to express my appreciation to many colleagues at WRI for their varied contributions: Jodi Nelson, Kurt Hupé, Katy Perry, Hyacinth Billings, Kathleen Courrier, Jonathan Lash, Keith Kozloff, Tom Fox, Bob Livernash, Al Hammond, Walt Reid, Paul Faeth, Tanvi Nagpal, and Robbie Nichols. Finally, on behalf of WRI I thank the MacArthur, Rockefeller, and Ford Foundations, the Pew Charitable Trusts, and the Netherlands Ministry of Foreign Affairs for their generous support for this effort.

R.R.

Foreword

At any given moment, it is hard to gauge how a burgeoning population is affecting a nation's economic prospects, poverty levels, and environment. Only over decades does the signal-to-noise ratio become clear—which is why this retrospective look at a study unprecedented in its era is so significant.

In the late 1960s, when India's population stood at about 500 million, the forward-looking *Second India Study* asked how India could cope with demands for more food, land, water, jobs, schooling, and energy as its population doubled by the year 2000. With the creation of a "second India" nearly completed, a research team of eminent Indian experts and Dr. Robert Repetto, WRI vice president and senior economist, compared the study's forecasts with the actual effects of a rapid population doubling to develop a better understanding of the interrelationship among demographic change, economic growth, environmental stress and government policy.

Published on the eve of the International Conference on Population and Development in Cairo, *"Second India" Revisited* brings accurate data and objective analyses to bear on the quandaries and questions that will dominate the Cairo conference. Passions tend to run high when people with vastly different perspectives grapple with the convoluted knot that binds poverty, population growth, development, and environmental damage together. We hope Cairo conference-goers will find use for this dispassionate exploration of how all these factors interacted in India over the past 25 years.

Though limited to one nation, these analyses can inform planning for the more populous world of the next century. Demographers project that India's population will double again before it stabilizes, adding a Third and a Fourth India—and that many other developing countries will trace similar growth curves over the next few decades. Seeing where the *Second India Study* was right—and wrong—can help nations facing steep population increases to chart a course for reducing poverty and limiting ecological damages in the near term and, eventually, stabilizing their populations. The report also identifies policy changes that can help countries reconcile inevitable population increases with the need for development and environmental protection.

The analyses set forth in *"Second India" Revisited* advance and complement those of such recent WRI studies as *Population Growth, Poverty, and Environmental Stress: Frontier Migration in the Philippines and Costa Rica* and *Agricultural Policy and Sustainability: Case Studies from India, Chile, the Philippines, and the United States*. To carry this work forward on a global scale, WRI is working with the Brookings Institution and the Santa Fe Institute to determine how societies everywhere might become sustainable by the year 2050. In collaboration with colleagues from many countries, the 2050 Project's research team has envisioned a sustainable future for countries and regions and is now surveying the policy interventions needed during this decade to make that future possible.

We would like to thank The John D. and Catherine T. MacArthur Foundation, The Rockefeller Foundation, The Ford Foundation, The Pew Charitable Trusts, and the Netherlands Ministry of Foreign Affairs, whose generous support made this study possible. To all these institutions, we owe a debt of gratitude.

Jonathan Lash
President
World Resources Institute

Collaborators

Dr. Bina Agarwal
Professor of Economics, Institute of Economic Growth, University of Delhi, Delhi

Dr. Alaka Basu
Professor of Economics, Institute of Economic Growth, University of Delhi, Delhi

Dr. B. Bowonder
Dean of Research, Administrative Staff College of India, Hyderabad

Dr. Willem C. F. Bussink
Consultant on macroeconomic development, population and poverty, The Hague, The Netherlands

Dr. Kanchan Chopra
Professor of Economics, Institute of Economic Growth, University of Delhi, Delhi

Dr. Om Prakash Mathur
Professor of Housing & Urban Economics, National Institute of Public Finance & Policy, New Delhi

Dr. R. K. Pachauri
Director, Tata Energy Research Institute, New Delhi

Dr. Kirit Parikh
Director, Indira Gandhi Institute of Development Research, Bombay

Dr. K. Srinivasan
Director Emeritus, International Institute of Population Studies, Bombay

Dr. A. Vaidyanathan
Former Member, Planning Commission, Government of India and Professor Emeritus, Madras Institute of Development Studies, Madras

I. Overview

A. Background to the Study

In September 1994, at the World Population Conference in Cairo, delegates, scientists, and concerned citizens from around the world will meet to consider how poverty, illiteracy and inequality keep birth and death rates high. They will debate the consequences of an almost inevitable doubling of world population for the environment and for human wellbeing. The debate will be contentious; the outcome, uncertain. New perspectives on gender inequality and reproductive health have come to the fore, but the main issues are still those that were argued at the second World Population Conference in Mexico City in 1984 and at the first World Population Conference in Bucharest in 1974. Little has been resolved, partly because value judgments, ideological leanings, and assumptions conditioned by economic status, geography, race, and gender affect people's perspectives on population issues so strongly.

Almost twenty-five years ago, hoping to promote a dispassionate examination of issues that were no less contentious then, the Ford Foundation assembled a group of notable Indian scholars to assess the implications of the doubling of India's population that demographers in 1970 considered inevitable. Then as now, India was considered by many to be one of the critical grounds on which the dynamics of population, poverty, and resource scarcity would be played out. Radically different diagnoses and prognoses were being offered. The Government of India's Planning Commission had just offered a medium-term development plan that foresaw much faster growth in agricultural production and income, rapid poverty alleviation, and a fifty-percent drop in the birth rate. A notable expatriate agricultural expert, impressed with the success of high-yielding rice and wheat varieties, proclaimed "Something fundamental and dynamic, with far reaching consequences, has been introduced into the Indian agricultural scene since 1965…The quantum change in technology has been added to a foodgrain production which was already growing at a rate of 2.5 percent annually since Independence. Therefore, it is difficult to imagine a growth rate of foodgrain production over the next decade of less than 3.5 percent annual trend…We feel that a 5 percent rate is most probable" (Cummings [1969]).

Speaking at the same time, however, equally confident observers predicted disaster—India's inability to feed its growing population: according to Paul Ehrlich's, *The Population Bomb*: "It now seems inevitable that death through starvation will be at least one factor in the coming increase in the death rate" (Ehrlich [1968], 69). In a widely read book, William and Paul Paddock took an even more alarmist position: "All evidence shows that there is no possibility that sufficient new technology will be developed through research in time to avert widespread famine" (Paddock & Paddock [1967], 78). "…today's trends show that it will be beyond the resources of the U.S. to keep famine out of India during the 1970s. Indian agriculture is too antiquated. Its present government is too inefficient to inaugurate long-term agricultural development programs. Its population tidal wave is too overwhelming, more than 11,500,000 are added each year to the current half-billion population" (Paddock & Paddock [1967], 217).

IT'S JUST GOING TO CONTINUE AND CONTINUE

Drawing by Stevenson © 1975
The New Yorker Magazine, Inc.

Amid polarized debates of this sort, the eight-volume report sponsored by the Ford Foundation in India, the *Second India Study*, was the most comprehensive and systematic effort up to that time to foresee the consequences of population growth—

for economic development, poverty alleviation, food supply, and natural resource use. There were individual studies on demography, urbanization, the economy, agriculture, water, energy, industry, and services. There were also an overview report and separate regional studies. Each author considered events up through 1970, prospects and constraints relevant to the sector, and constructed several plausible scenarios for the future up through the year 2000. All authors tried as best they could to link developments across sectors.

Now that the doubling of India's population is within sight, WRI has joined another team of eminent Indian experts to compare the scenarios of the *Second India Study* with actual developments. The first objective in reassessing the *Second India Study* is to see to what extent even the most extensive efforts to foresee the interplay of demographic, economic, and ecological change succeeded. Today, dogmatic pronouncements, both optimistic and pessimistic, about the consequences of future population growth still abound. Is such dogmatism justified? Can even serious scholars accurately foresee what adaptations to current constraints will emerge, or what new problems will materialize? What are the pitfalls of extrapolating current trends into the future?

The authors of the original *Second India Study* were by no means oblivious to the perils in their way. Dr. Hannan Ezekiel, who wrote the overview study, cautioned: "The world of futurology is full of the wreckage of projections that have been completely disproved by actual developments. The main problem arises from the fact that futurology finds it impossible to deal with large and unpredictable shocks to the economy which make nonsense of the assumptions on which all projections have to be made, and, in particular, of the basic assumption of continuity which underlies the entire process of projection-making" (Ezekiel [1975], *Overview*, 4).

In some areas, this assumption of continuity was amply justified. India continues to wrestle with many of the same problems today that were obvious in 1970. Managing water, forests, and other natural resources that form India's communal endowment is just as challenging today as it was then. In fact, Indian policy is once again devolving authority and responsibility to local government and community organizations, reversing a decades-long centralizing trend. In urban areas, providing housing, water, sanitation, and other basic services to an expanding city population has proven to be every bit the problem that the *Second India Study* foresaw. So has been the challenge of generating jobs for a labor force doubling in size. In these respects, among others, the *Second India Study*'s vision was accurate.

However, there were external shocks that have fundamentally changed the course of India's economy, which the *Second India Study* could not clearly foresee: the oil price shocks that made India's energy-intensive heavy industrialization pattern irretrievably uneconomic; the accelerating globalization of the international economy, which invalidated India's inward-looking import substitution strategy; the collapse of the Soviet Union and the switch to rapid market-oriented growth in China, which undermined India's commitment to central planning and state-dominated development and has led to the economic reforms initiated in the 1980s and still continuing. The *Second India Study* volumes traced out the implications of various assumptions about the future, but one assumption that was not questioned—although it had the most far-reaching consequences—was that India would continue under the centrally planned economic regime that had been established in the 1950s and 1960s. The gradual liberalization of that regime has been one of the factors enabling India's economic growth to accelerate over the last decade.

By and large, developments since the *Second India Study* was undertaken twenty years ago fall within the range of scenarios the authors thought plausible. In general, progress in industrial and agricultural growth, poverty alleviation, and demographic transition has been nearer the pessimistic end of the range, but during the 1980s the pace of development quickened significantly. In this sense, the middle ground taken by the *Second India Study* turned out to be the safer position.

However, there have been plenty of surprises and a few mysteries over two decades of experience. Among the surprises:

- By 1991, fertility rates in the South Indian states of Kerala and Tamil Nadu had reached replacement level or below, while rates in much of North India still exceeded five over the average woman's lifetime.

- Over India as a whole, natural fertility—the number of births a non-contracepting woman would experience in a lifetime—had risen from about six to about nine, a 50-percent increase over roughly two decades.

- Despite the continuing shrinkage in agricultural land per person in the countryside, by the late 1980s the percentage of people below the poverty line was lower in rural villages than in cities.

- Throughout most of the period there were shortages of coal and coal-based electricity, though domestic reserves of coal are ample. By contrast, reserves and production of petroleum and natural gas, which were thought to be scarce, have greatly increased.

There are other developments that remain mysterious, not well understood or explained even by Indian experts. For example, the percentage of Indian households with monthly expenditures high enough to permit them to buy a nutritionally adequate supply of calories rose, from 45 percent in 1973 to 61 percent in 1988. In India, this is how the poverty line is defined. However, an increasing share of these households above the poverty line are apparently *not* consuming a nutritionally adequate amount of calories, even though they can afford to. They are spending their greater resources on non-food items and on relatively expensive foodstuffs instead of on basic cereals and pulses. The percentage of such households increased from 12 to 37 percent of the total between 1978 and 1988.

Equally mysterious is the rise in real wages in India in both rural and urban areas and in virtually all regions. Real wages rose not only in the 1980s, when growth was quick, but also in the 1970s, when growth was slow. Yet, during both decades, neither agriculture nor factory industry generated enough new jobs even to keep pace with the growth in the labor force, let alone to cut into the huge backlog of underemployment. The explanation, still to be found, must lie in the unexpected vigor of job creation in the huge unorganized non-farm sector, in which most Indians actually work.

The *Second India Study* anticipated some problems that have not materialized. The authors greatly overestimated the resource requirements of India's economic development. They discounted the impact of new technologies that would be adopted, even in India's relatively closed economy. For example, virtually the entire steel industry converted from open hearth to electric arc furnaces, greatly reducing energy requirements. The cement industry shifted from wet to dry processes, with similar results. Also, the emphasis on heavy industry characteristic of India's development strategy in the 1960s was moderated. As a result, much less steel was needed for machine building, railway construction, and the like. Fewer railway lines and cars were needed to carry coal and less coal was needed to feed steam boilers and industrial furnaces. Even though India's economic policies during the period provided few incentives to conserve resources, structural and technological change nonetheless worked to that end. As a result, the environmental impacts and capital requirements of India's growth were substantially less than they would have been under *Second India Study* scenarios.

It is also true that problems have materialized that were not foreseen. In agriculture, for example, despite the optimism generated in the 1960s by the success of high-yielding wheat and rice seed varieties, an extensive agricultural research effort in India has been unable to demonstrate continuing yield improvements over the 1970s and 1980s for major crops. Newly released seeds and agronomic input packages tested on farmers' fields have failed to show upward yield trends in the past two decades. Whether this represents de-

---

Despite the optimism generated in the 1960s by the success of high-yielding wheat and rice seed varieties, an extensive agricultural research effort in India has been unable to demonstrate continuing yield improvements over the 1970s and 1980s for major crops.

---

terioration in underlying soil fertility, weaknesses in the agricultural research effort, or genetic limitations in the plant materials available for use, is not well known. Whatever the cause, average farm yields continue to rise, but toward a static ceiling of demonstrated research results.

Overall, the record of the *Second India Study* teaches both the value of serious efforts to look ahead at the implications of massive population expansion and the need for a certain humility in making predictions. The *Study* did identify many of the key challenges that India would face and raised some of the key policy issues that policymakers needed to confront—and, by and large, have confronted over the succeeding two decades.

B. The Main Trends

Another objective in reexamining India's experience, using the *Second India Study* as a benchmark, was to trace out the key interactions of population growth, economic development, and environmental stress over 20 years. The opportunity was unique because only over a span of decades can these underlying dynamics be discerned amid the short-term shocks and adjustments of economic development.

The conclusions of the *Second India Study*, though varied, were basically optimistic that poverty and population growth could be reduced despite India's limited financial and natural resources. However, the authors emphasized that doing so depended not so much on the availability of technology as on solving difficult and long-standing social and institutional problems.

These judgments were basically correct. The disasters predicted by Malthusian pessimists have not happened and India has continued to develop economically over the past two decades. But progress has been toward the low end of *Second India Study* projections, certainly much slower than hoped in the Government of India's various Five-Year Development Plans, and slower than that observed in many other large developing countries in Asia.

The population growth rate between 1970 and 1990 was only very slightly lower than it had been during the previous two decades: 2.1 percent per year compared to 2.2 percent. Near constancy in the growth rate masked the underlying demographic transition: birth rates and death rates did fall—each by about 25 percent. The percentage of couples using contraceptives rose from 10 to 40 percent over the period, largely through the efforts of the government-supported family planning program. Per thousand of population, health personnel and clinical facilities expanded by 50 percent or more. However, life expectancy in India in 1990 was about 60 years—still substantially lower than in the developing regions of East and Southeast Asia. Although infant mortality rates have fallen and the diseases of old age now take a comparatively higher toll, poverty-related diseases stemming from malnutrition and exposure to respiratory and gastro-intestinal infections still predominate.

Economic growth has also been toward the low end of *Second India Study* projections and beneath that achieved elsewhere in Asia, but at least as rapid as in the rest of the developed or developing world. Between 1970–71 and 1990–91, GDP growth in constant prices averaged 4 percent, but this masks a substantial step-up from 3.5 percent in the 1970s to 5.3 percent in the 1980s. Contrary to some economic theories, India was able to raise

its household savings rate significantly, despite continuing rapid population growth. Economic growth allowed a slight reduction in the number of people in India living below the poverty line, despite the addition of three hundred million people to the population over this period, and despite little change in the distribution of income between rich and poor. However, according to the latest estimates, over 300 million people, almost 40 percent of the total population, still were below the poverty line in 1987–88. These two trends are interrelated: slow progress in reducing poverty has retarded the fall in birth and death rates, and the near constancy in the rate of population growth has retarded progress in eliminating poverty.

Agricultural production has continued to rise at virtually the same trend growth rate observed during the preceding twenty years, even though the net cultivated area hasn't increased in the past two decades. The Green Revolution didn't fail, but neither has it produced a quantum increase in the growth of foodgrains output. Rather, it allowed production to continue expanding by increasing yields, even after the limits of cultivable acreage had been approached. Supplies have been adequate to meet *market* demand and to improve the diet of the average person somewhat, though poverty still consigns hundreds of millions of Indians to malnutrition. Foodgrains production per capita has increased by only 5.4 percent despite 20 years of agricultural development efforts. The Green Revolution really took hold in the alluvial river basins where tubewell irrigation during winter was possible. Dryland agriculture has lagged further behind, so regional disparities in rural incomes have increased.

Throughout most of the period, neither the pace of growth nor the pattern of development has provided the growing numbers of jobs needed to absorb the expanding labor force and cut into the backlog of underemployment in rural and urban India. In the Green Revolution areas, pumpsets, tractors, and chemicals have replaced labor in farm operations, limiting the growth of farm employment. In lagging agricultural areas, shrinking land-man ratios have exacerbated existing labor surpluses. A growing percentage of the rural labor force has had recourse to casual wage employment off the farm, some of it generated by governmental rural employment and other targeted anti-poverty schemes. In urban areas, employment in large and medium-sized industries has also grown much more slowly than output, which itself has increased more slowly than in other developing Asian economies. Capital-labor and capital-output ratios rose in most Indian industries over the period. However, especially as economic growth accelerated during the 1980s, rising real wages in most parts of the country seems to have indicated a pick-up in labor demand.

In most respects, India's environment has deteriorated markedly since the *Second India Study* was written. In canal-irrigated areas, dams are rapidly silting up because of deforestation upstream, and millions of hectares of farmland have become waterlogged or salinized because water has been applied improperly. In large areas where tubewell development has been intensive, water tables are falling; in coastal areas, salt water is invading and ruining the aquifers, depriving tens of millions of people of drinking and irrigation water. In areas of intensive farming, deficiencies in organic matter and micronutrients have emerged and limit crop yields.

In the uncultivated parts of rural India, two thirds of the total area, overharvesting of fuelwood and overgrazing of livestock—combined with unsustainable rates of commercial exploitation—have devegetated the landscape. Neither central nor state government authorities have been able to ration access to these communal resources effectively and equitably. Large-scale soil erosion and disruption of hydrological flows have resulted. Increasing shortages of fuelwood, fodder, and other useful products of India's commons have added to the deprivations of the rural poor, especially women, who are most dependent on those resources. Most of India's varied native ecosystems now exist only in remnant patches, under great pressure from surrounding populations and commercial interests. Shrinking habitats have reduced the numbers and the ranges of India's magnificent and diverse plant, animal and bird populations, endangering many.

Most of India's varied native ecosystems now exist only in remnant patches, under great pressure from surrounding populations and commercial interests.

Although governments have invested heavily to provide greater access to safe drinking water and other basic infrastructure, the urban environment has also deteriorated in many respects. The urban population has grown twice as fast as rural numbers have. Because job opportunities have not kept pace with the growing labor force in cities, the numbers of the urban poor have grown by one third over twenty years. Living in makeshift huts in squatter settlements without proper sanitation and waste disposal, most poor city-dwellers are heavily exposed to water pollution and communicable diseases. Air pollution from industrial emissions and from vehicle exhausts that still contain lead is a worsening problem, especially for malnourished children with chronic respiratory infections.

C. Vicious and Virtuous Circles

Participants in the original *Second India Study* saw the diverging paths towards India's future, some leading toward development and prosperity but others leading to deeper poverty and degradation. They emphasized that steps in either direction would be self-reinforcing, propelling the nation down one path or the other. As Hannan Ezekiel put it, "I was deeply impressed by two things. One was the existence of vicious or virtuous circles of interaction having profound implications for the likely state of the economy at the end of the period. The other was the critical role of policy in determining whether these relationships would, in fact, operate to produce vicious or virtuous circles…."

The overall interplay between population, poverty, and resource availability was described in such terms. Here is his description of the dark scenario: "Income will grow slowly. Population will grow rapidly. Per capita income will, therefore, grow very slowly. This will have a negative impact on family planning efforts…Also, savings ratios will not rise and may even fall…Industrial growth will be slow. Growth in industrial employment will be even slower…The existing land hunger will increase. Further subdivision and fragmentation of land will take place. Propagation of new techniques of cultivation will become more difficult…In this context, talk of social justice will be mere nonsense. The proportion of the population below the poverty line will certainly increase…The employment situation will also worsen and it may well be that the ability of the socioeconomic system to cover it up in various forms…will prove to be inadequate…Communal, caste, regional or economic groups will fight with one another with increasing bitterness in order to obtain for themselves a share of the limited real resources, income and employment available in the country" (Ezekiel [1975], *Overview*, 189–190).

While this dark vision finds some reflection in events in India since the early 1970s, the striking trend is the increasing differentiation of development patterns. While some regions stagnate, others move briskly ahead. In fact, both virtuous and vicious circles are evident in India's diverse regions. In Kerala, for example, women have long enjoyed better status and opportunity. Women obtained more education and married later. They gained greater access to professional and other socially sanctioned employment, which cemented their position and authority within the household. For all these reasons, contraceptive use and fertility decline took hold early in Kerala. This, in turn, allowed women to pursue education and career more easily, and increased their social status and economic opportunity. Today, 85 percent of Kerala's women are literate, the infant mortality rate is comparable to that in New York City and fertility is below replacement level.

By contrast, in northern and northwestern states, such as Rajasthan, women typically married outside their own villages and were secluded within their husbands' household, virtually excluded from paid employment except in extreme circumstances. Status came from mothering sons. Girls received little education, married early, and commenced childbearing. With little autonomy or education, most women's opportunities outside the home were virtually *nil*. Thus, their social status remained low, and few girls received more than rudimentary education. Marriage age stayed low, and birth rates continued high. In Rajasthan today, only 20 percent of women are literate, only 30 percent of married couples practice contraception, and the average married woman has five to six children.

Other vicious and virtuous circles affect India's environment and resources. The British colonial government assumed authority over almost all of India's forests and uncultivated regions, all but abrogating the traditional rights and regimes of village communities, tribal societies, and other groups that had used these resources—more or less sustainably—for generations. After Independence, succeeding central and state governments were largely unable to restrain access to this vast domain in the face of rising populations and demands for raw materials. When demands surpassed sustainable yields, a cycle of depletion and degradation was set in motion. Seeing others taking the increasingly scarce resources without stint, none saw reason to restrain their own demands. Thus, overexploited stocks and harvests shrank as population and demands on what remained intensified. As the value of communal resources deteriorated, village leaders increasingly withdrew from attempts to manage what remained, leaving the rural poor to glean what they could from the ever-shrinking woodlands and pastures.

In a few areas, the cycle has been interrupted and reversed. Communities assured of equitable and exclusive use of the commons have limited overexploitation and cooperated in rehabilitation programs. Investments in restoration have raised productivity, diminishing the pressure to overexploit the resource. Higher returns have provided the resources for further investments, leading to further increases in productivity. Although only in exceptional instances has the notorious "tragedy of the commons" thus been reversed, these promising examples have led to a needed reexamination of development policies.

D. The Primacy of Institutions and of Policies

The authors of the *Second India Study* made clear their views that India had the power to choose options that would generate employment, reduce poverty, accelerate the demographic transition, and avert resource crises. They emphasized that neither the technology available at that time nor the availability of natural resources precluded India from raising living standards for a doubled population. The agricultural technologies needed to double yields and production on both dry and irrigated farmland existed then. India also possessed enough energy resources to meet the needs of cities, industries, and villages.

According to the *Second India Study*, by choosing policies that spurred rapid employment growth, government could deal effectively with poverty and malnutrition within the economic system, rather than by attempting to mitigate the failures of economic development through special anti-poverty interventions. By reducing poverty and investing heavily in education and health, the government could ensure the success of the family planning program and accelerate the demographic transition. By promoting community woodlots, biogas plants, and rural electrification, the government could provide enough fuel and forage to relieve pressure on India's common property resources. By better managing water resources and by integrating surface and groundwater systems, India could expand its irrigated area without environmental damage. The question was whether India would choose these successful options.

A look back over the past twenty years confirms the correctness of this point of view. Neither technologies nor resources have been the intractable problems. Rather, where development has faltered, the stumbling blocks have usually been institutional and policy related. The key issue has often turned out to be that of creating mechanisms, whether through market incentives, community organizations, or other means of governance, for bringing the interests of the individual into line with those of the broader community. Where this has happened, the circles have been virtuous; where it has not, the circles have been vicious and the dynamics destructive and unsustainable.

In family planning, the government has continued to emphasize the technologies of birth control, first the IUD, then male and female sterilization. An extensive service network has been constructed to provide these technologies throughout India, with substantial impact on those ready to terminate child-bearing. However, what has become increasingly evident is the importance of social institutions that afford women social status, autonomy, and opportunity—not only to regulate their fertility but to satisfy their health, economic and social needs as well. In parts of India, where women can fulfill these needs, their own interests in family planning coincide with those of the larger community.

In other realms, similar findings emerge. For example, persistent energy shortages have indeed robbed India of badly needed output and employment, depriving the urban and rural poor alike. But, neither technology nor natural resources have been constraining. India has large coal reserves and far more oil and gas than was suspected twenty-five years ago. One reason for scarcities of commercial fuels has been the failure to price energy high enough to ration demand and generate funds for reinvestment. Another reason has been continued reliance on inefficient public sector monopolies. In rural areas, renewable energy technologies and potential biomass resources have been available, but too few resources have been allocated to meet the energy needs of the rural poor, and too few community governance structures have been built and supported to reverse the notorious tragedy of the commons.

In agriculture, India has successfully promoted the use of its underground water resources and the new Green Revolution technology to meet its food requirements. Where farmers could invest in electric or diesel powered tubewells, and control their own water supplies, the use of modern agricultural technologies has paid off, and farmers have rapidly increased their yields and incomes. Local water markets have emerged through which those without wells can share in the benefits. By contrast, in large canal irrigation systems, where the interests of farmers come into conflict, politicized irrigation administrations have been unable to allocate water efficiently and equitably. Compared to tubewells, canal irrigation still remains typically unreliable or inadequate and has increased agricultural yields much less.

Moreover, because groundwater exploitation was heavily subsidized on a first-come, first-served basis, the better-off farmers were allowed control of an immensely valuable resource at virtually no cost, and an opportunity was missed to allocate more rural assets and income to small farmers and agricultural workers. Where water scarcities emerged, the absence of any effective means to limit the individual farmer's withdrawals has led to depletion or ecological damage. By concentrating its fiscal resources heavily on the alluvial areas where tubewells were advantageous, the government put the lagging dryland and flood-prone regions at a disadvantage, allowing rural income disparities to widen.

The evidence that has emerged in India over the 20 years since the *Second India Study* was carried out suggests that a rapid demographic transition, poverty alleviation, and development can occur simultaneously even in poor and populous countries. But unsustainable spirals of population growth, environmental degradation and impoverishment are also possible. Population growth such as India's makes it harder to reduce underemployment and poverty, raise educational levels and environmental quality, or provide adequate infrastructure and basic services, but it doesn't make these tasks impossible. The key determinants of success seem to lie in the social framework, broadly conceived to include the system of norms, economic arrangements, policies, and institutions of governance.

II. Population Change in India: A 20-Year Perspective

The expected population doubling that motivated the *Second India Study* will have occurred by the year 2007 (Bowonder, *Population*, 15, Table 15). The 1991 census counted 846 million Indians, almost as many as in the highest *Second India Study* projection of 849 million and 32 million people more than in the lowest. By mid-1994, the Indian population had increased further, to about 900 million. The population increase since 1971, when it stood at 548 million, has been larger than the total increase in the six earlier decades of the 20th century (Srinivasan, 1). In fact, if the people added to India's population since 1971 inhabited a country of their own, it would be the world's third most populous country, smaller only than China and India itself.

Although the growth rate during the past decade—2.12 percent annually—has declined slightly from the 2.20 percent rate experienced during the 1970s, in much of India (including the states of Andhra Pradesh, Himachal Pradesh, Bihar, Jammu Kashmir, Punjab, Rajasthan, Uttar Pradesh, and Karnataka), the population growth rate is still increasing, and the rate of increase nationwide since 1971 remains higher than that experienced between 1951 and 1971. As a consequence, India's population remains young: 36 percent of the population is under 15 years old, compared to 42 percent in 1971. The generation of women entering their reproductive years during each decade continues to be much larger than the previous cohort, continuing the momentum of population growth even as the number of births per woman falls. Therefore, demographers project that India's population will double again before it stabilizes, adding a Third and Fourth India to the 1971 population totals (World Bank [1993], Table 26). *(See Figure 1.)*

A. Changing Mortality Patterns

Although population growth rates for India as a whole have changed only slightly over the past two decades, both birth and death rates have fallen. The *Second India Study* assumed that by 1991 life expectancy at birth would have reached 60 years, and the 2.5 year disadvantage in life expectancy that females suffered in 1971 would have been largely eliminated. The study predicted that rapid post-war gains from the control of famines and communicable diseases would be difficult to sustain since mortality gains would thereafter depend more on improvements in nutritional intake, primary health care in rural areas, and the provision of safe drinking water and sanitation.

This tempered optimism has largely been vindicated. Life expectancy at birth had crossed the 60-year mark by 1991, 59.5 for men and 60.5 for women. *(See Figure 2.)* Among countries at comparable levels of per capita income, only China has a high life expectancy. However, slower growth in income and foodgrains production than the *Second India Study* projected has meant slower progress in reducing poverty and malnutrition. Sickness and death stemming from malnutrition, low resistance to infectious diseases, unsanitary

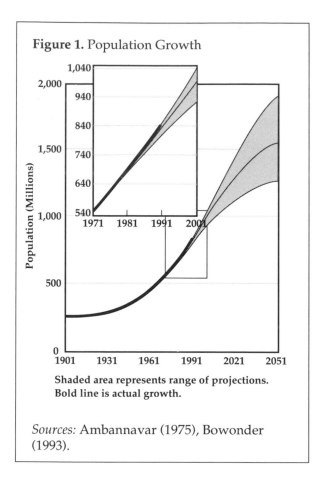

Figure 1. Population Growth

Population (Millions)

Shaded area represents range of projections.
Bold line is actual growth.

Sources: Ambannavar (1975), Bowonder (1993).

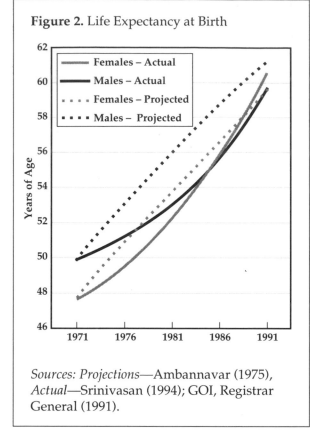

Figure 2. Life Expectancy at Birth

Females – Actual
Males – Actual
Females – Projected
Males – Projected

Years of Age

Sources: Projections—Ambannavar (1975), *Actual*—Srinivasan (1994); GOI, Registrar General (1991).

living conditions, and inadequate medical attention are still common among India's poor (GOI, Central Bureau of Health Intelligence [1991]).

Since birth rates also remain high in much of India, mortality among underage, overage, unhealthy, malnourished, or poorly attended mothers has continued to be high. Maternal mortality rates in India are still about 50 times higher than in high-income countries, and since the typical Indian woman experiences around five pregnancies, her lifetime risk is very great. Female mortality rates during the peak reproductive years exceed those of males. Most maternal and neonatal deaths could be prevented through better care. In rural areas, only about one third of deliveries are attended by trained personnel in equipped facilities—although this ranges from 77 percent in Kerala to only 1.5 percent in Rajasthan (UNICEF, 12–17).

The infant mortality rate remained about 130 deaths per 1,000 live births from 1970 to 1978, for reasons not yet well understood. Thereafter, however, it has improved steadily to 80 per thousand in 1991. This timing coincides with the acceleration in growth of per capita incomes during the 1980s, and also with the shift in development expenditures toward anti-poverty programs. However, neonatal mortality rates—deaths during the first four weeks of life—have improved only slightly. Prematurity and low birthweights from maternal malnutrition and anaemia, short intervals between births, and the inadequacy of medical attention before and during delivery, including the lack of tetanus immunization, all contribute to high neonatal mortality. Infant mortality rates continue to be substantially higher in rural areas and in urban slums, where poverty is high, environmental conditions are poor, and medical care is deficient. Mortality differentials between leading and backward regions are sharp (UNICEF, 31–33).

Child mortality was reduced substantially over the period by better nutrition, expanded immunization, and the better medical attention that has come with urbanization, the expanded network of primary health centers, and the more widespread educational attainment of mothers. Children of better educated mothers have markedly higher survival chances. Deaths to children under five accounted for nearly half of all deaths in 1971, but less than two fifths by 1986 and close to one-third by 1991 (World Bank [1993], Table A6). Although the majority of children still experience moderate or mild malnutrition, including debilitating vitamin, iron, or iodine deficiencies, the percentage of children suffering from severe malnutrition fell by half from the mid-70s to the late 1980s, in part because of governmental food distribution and child-feeding programs (Bowonder, *Food*, 20).

However, in the North Indian Hindi-speaking states of Rajasthan, Haryana, Uttar Pradesh, and Madhya Pradesh, survival chances are considerably worse for girls than boys once infancy is passed. *(See Figure 3.)* This is telling evidence of a gender bias against females: male infants are greeted with rejoicing as a source of future family support and strength; female births are regarded as misfortunes. Little boys are given priority in feeding and medical expenditure; little girls must often make do with what's left over. In contrast to most other countries, India's population contains increasingly fewer females than males: 927 per thousand males in 1991, compared to 930 in 1971. In the large North Indian states where women are sequestered and discriminated against, including Bihar and the Punjab as well as those mentioned above, this sex imbalance is pronounced. Women's survival chances are lower and they may simply not be counted at census time (Basu, 21; Srinivasan, 6). Health surveys consistently find that when women get ill, they typically wait much longer before seeking medical help, if they do at all.

Nonetheless, as life expectancies have risen over the past 20 years, signs that India is entering the "epidemiological transition" have appeared (Omran, [1975], cited in Srinivasan, 11). Deaths of those under five have fallen as a proportion of all deaths, and deaths of those over 40 have steadily risen (Srinivasan, 12). This trend reflects the growing importance of non-infectious diseases, such as stroke, heart diseases, and cancers, as well as accidents and injuries—as the toll of child-killing respiratory and gastroenteritis infections gradually diminishes. Improvements in children's nutrition, immunization, and access to primary health care are important factors behind this transition (Srinivasan, 13).

B. Falling Birth Rates

Paralleling this fall in death rates, the crude birth rate has declined by approximately 25 percent over two decades. Fertility decline in India has been slower than in other large Asian countries, such as Indonesia, Thailand, and China, but faster than in the neighboring countries of Pakistan, Bangladesh, and Nepal. The pace of decline has not been constant; rather, periods of falling rates were interrupted by years of stability. The birth rate remained almost constant from 1973 through 1985 at around 32–35, then dropped to 30 by 1991. The total fertility rate (the average number of children born per woman) declined rather slowly from 5.2 in 1971 to 4.5 in 1984, but has since then fallen briskly to 3.6 children per woman in 1991. *(See Figure 4.)*

About 80 percent of the overall decline is the consequence of more widespread use of birth control devices by married women. Increases in the average age at which women marry—the result of urbanization, women's increasing school attendance, and the spread of modern attitudes—have reduced the birth rate about half as much. The increase in the proportion of women of peak reproductive age in the total population, the consequence of past population increases, worked in the other direction, pushing fertility upward (Srinivasan, 19–21).

A key linkage with socioeconomic development that has slowed India's fertility decline has been the rise of natural fertility, the number of births that a woman would have if she used no

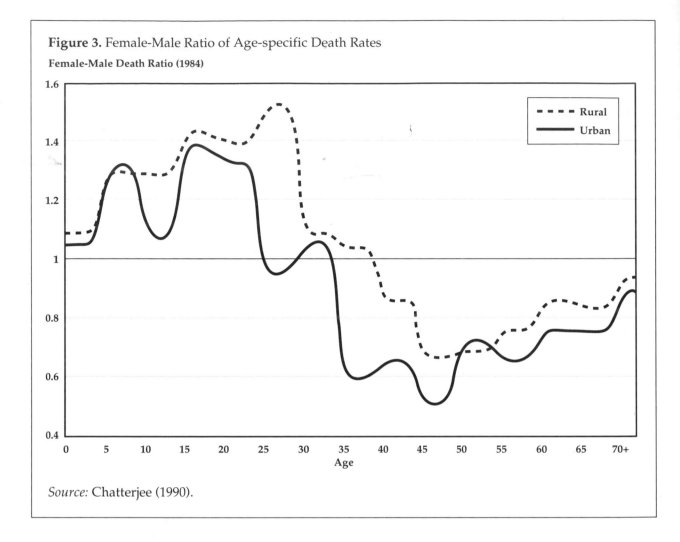

Figure 3. Female-Male Ratio of Age-specific Death Rates

Female-Male Death Ratio (1984)

Source: Chatterjee (1990).

India's decline in birth rates has occurred against a 25 to 30 percent rise in natural fertility, a consequence of economic development.

contraceptives. Natural fertility in India has historically been only about 6 live births per lifetime—half the maximum observed in actual populations elsewhere. Despite the tradition of early and universal marriage, religious and cultural re-

strictions on sex, prohibitions against widows remarrying, prolonged breastfeeding, malnutrition, and the effects of malaria, tuberculosis and other diseases contributed to low natural fertility. Because many of these cultural practices have weakened, and because life expectancy and general health conditions have improved, natural fertility has risen substantially, to approximately 7 in the 1970s and 8 to 9 by 1991. Thus, India's decline in birth rates has occurred against a 25 to 30 percent rise in natural fertility, a consequence of economic development (Srinivasan, 19–21).

Evidence of rising natural fertility can be seen in the phenomenon of *rising* birth rates within marriage among women aged 15–25, ages at

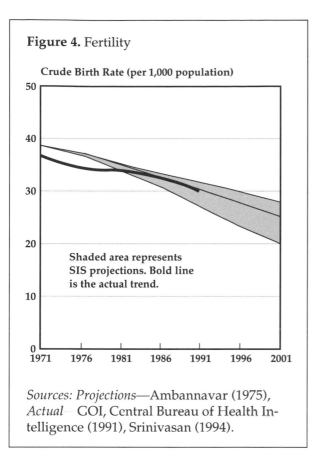

Figure 4. Fertility

Crude Birth Rate (per 1,000 population)

Shaded area represents
SIS projections. Bold line
is the actual trend.

Sources: Projections—Ambannavar (1975),
Actual—GOI, Central Bureau of Health Intelligence (1991), Srinivasan (1994).

in all sub-districts throughout the country. Both the government's own service statistics and independent household surveys indicate that contraceptive usage by modern methods has risen dramatically, from about 10 percent of married, potentially child-bearing women in 1970 to over 40 percent in 1990. Unfortunately, this increase in reported contraceptive usage has not been fully matched by a corresponding fall in marital fertility, either in the country as a whole or in individual states (Srinivasan, 30).

Critical problems facing the Indian family planning program were identified by the *Second India Study* in the early 1970s. They included overreliance on sterilization and other terminal birth control methods, preoccupation with achieving administrative targets for new family planning "acceptors" at the expense of attention to the quality of services and care, overuse of financial incentives as motivational instruments, and an excessively top-down bureaucratic approach to the program. Later in the 1970s, these criticisms proved prophetic. The family planning program underwent a phase in which overzealous, even coercive, methods were used to increase the number of sterilizations, and the popular backlash was partially responsible for the political defeat of the government in office.

Even today, 20 years after the *Second India Study*, it is remarkable that knowledgeable Indian observers direct virtually the same criticisms at the family planning program. Emphasizing sterilizations, mainly tubectomies, restricts the program largely to couples whose desired fertility is already completed, neglecting younger couples' needs for spacing and delaying fertility (Reddy, 315). Since most Indian families in regions where gender bias is strong still hope for more than one son to survive to adulthood, family sizes at which sterilization becomes acceptable are much higher than the replacement level of two children. Seeking to fulfill acceptor targets and using financial incentives for motivation diverts attention from providing high quality services that meet the full range of clients' reproductive and child health care needs (Bose [1988] cited in Jayasree et al., 23). Medical complications of sterilization operations are common,

which few Indian women would be deliberately limiting fertility. The Indian family planning program's focus on terminal methods of birth control—principally sterilization—and on stopping fertility after the desired family size has been achieved has accommodated this rise in marital fertility at young ages. New Indian wives are under considerable cultural pressure to deliver a son soon after marriage, and the family planning program's lack of emphasis on spacing births reflects and accommodates this orientation.

C. India's Family Planning Programs

India was the first country to launch an official family planning program, and has invested heavily to provide services to all. The Government of India has assumed financial responsibility for creating a standard supply network of clinics, mobile service facilities, medical and social workers many are sterilized who would be unlikely to bear more children anyway, and the reputation of the program suffers (Singh [1989]; Karkal, Malini, & Pandey [1989], 56, 68). Despite its substantial achievements, continuing weaknesses in India's family planning program are partly responsible for the relatively slow fertility decline.

D. Social and Cultural Determinants of Demographic Change

What has emerged most strongly over the past 20 years since the *Second India Study*, is the importance of social and cultural determinants in the demographic transition—especially women's place in the society (Basu, 2–6). This is demonstrated dramatically in the variations from state to state within India in both birth and death rates and in their close association with indicators of women's status—such as female literacy. Fertility has fallen in all Indian states and in villages as well as in cities, but regional differences have become more pronounced. In a socio-economically backward northern Indian state such as Uttar Pradesh, where traditional attitudes persist and women's status is low, the total fertility rate declined only from 5.9 to 5.1 between 1984 and 1991. In south India, fertility, which by 1984 had already dropped to 2.4 in Kerala and 3.3 in neighboring Tamil Nadu, fell further to 1.8 and 2.2, respectively. At these rates, the average woman only has enough births over her lifetime to replace herself.

The process of demographic transition is complex. In Tamil Nadu, which lags somewhat behind Kerala's progress in reducing infant mortality and raising female literacy, political commitment to promoting the small family norm has been strong, and relatively efficient state administration of health and family planning programs have reinforced this commitment. In the small coastal state of Goa, low fertility has been achieved through very rapid economic modernization and assimilation of Western ideas, including those on women's equality. In both states, as in Kerala, a range of contraceptive choices is readily available to potential users, and fairly high-quality and socially acceptable services are provided.

Kerala's experience stands out as demographically and socially distinct, although there is a clear demographic gradient from south India as a whole to the large Hindi-speaking states of the Indo-Gangetic plains, where fertility remains much higher. In 1991, Kerala's total fertility rate was lower than Sweden's or that of the United States. With an infant mortality rate of 17 and a birth rate below replacement level, Kerala has effectively completed the demographic transition that it began at least thirty years before the rest of India. Even today, the rest of India is experiencing levels of fertility and mortality that Kerala passed through 25 years ago, and average ages of marriage for women that Kerala surpassed 50 years ago (Srinivasan, Table 25).

What makes Kerala's experience so remarkable is that it is not an economically advanced region: the level of per capita income is relatively low, and the extent of urbanization and industrialization are only average. Moreover, Kerala's family planning program has adhered to national spending and staffing patterns: the availability of family planning clinics and sub-centers or of auxiliary nurse midwives, the principal family planning fieldworker, is no greater in Kerala, relative to population, than in the rest of India (Chaterjee, 108, Table 34). *(See Figure 5.)* Nonetheless, the decline in the total fertility rate between 1972 and 1991 was 60 percent, twice that of India as a whole.

Naturally, the secret of Kerala's demographic uniqueness has attracted a great deal of investigation. If it is not a greater family planning program effort, what has it been? Among the explanatory factors that have been advanced are Kerala's high population density, its relatively egalitarian socioeconomic structure, its political integration and administrative capabilities, and the fact that earlier declines in infant mortality and increases in school attendance had brought home to parents the high costs of large families in a region with few employment opportunities on family farmholdings. These explanations are not mutu-

Table 1. Time Lag of Other States from Kerala in Selected Demographic and Health Parameters—India, 1988

States	C B R	C D R	I M R	T F R	Mean Age at Marriage		Mortality		Deaths of Children 0–4 of Total Deaths (%)
					Male	Female	Neonatal	Postnatal	
Andhra Pradesh	12	16	28	25	>80	>80	>25	>20	>20
Assam	20	22	32	30	NA	NA	>25	>20	>20
Bihar	22	25	33	>50	>80	>25	>25	>20	>20
Gujarat	16	18	28	18	>80	40	>25	>20	>20
Haryana	20	16	28	30	>80	50	>25	>20	>20
Karnataka	15	14	23	14	30	40	>25	19	>20
Madhya Pradesh	22	28	37	30	>80	>80	>25	>20	>20
Maharashtra	16	16	28	14	60	50	>25	>20	>20
Orissa	19	22	38	28	60	40	>25	19	>20
Punjab	15	16	18	14	60	10	22	>20	>20
Rajasthan	20	28	28	>50	>80	>80	>25	>20	>20
Tamil Nadu	3	14	22	12	20	10	>25	19	18
Uttar Pradesh	22	25	38	>50	>80	50	>25	>20	>20
West Bengal	15	16	28	14	30	40	>25	>20	>20
India	18	20	28	28	50	50	>25	>20	>20
Kerala (base values)	20.3	6.4	28	2.3	27.2	21.8	18	9.7	12.66

Note: Base year for all variables is 1988 except 1981 for mean age at marriage.
Source: Srinivasan (1993).

ally exclusive, and all may contain a grain of truth. However, it has become increasingly evident that the most important factor has been the uniquely favorable position that women have traditionally held in Keralan society, and still enjoy by comparison to the severe disadvantages women face in much of the rest of India (Mahadevan [1989], Basu [1993]).

Traditional Indian attitudes have held that women are to be protected and honored, particularly as mothers, but not that women were to be independent. Women were to serve their husbands and to obey their in-laws. In Northern India, women typically marry outside their own villages and clans, and therefore typically go as strangers to their husbands' houses. They are expected to defer to their husband's parents and older brothers and sisters-in-law. Women gain status and economic security over time as the mothers of their husbands' sons (Karkal, Malini, & Pandey [1989]; Mahadevan [1989]).

Traditionally, women lived in seclusion within the household and covered their heads and faces from the gaze of outsiders or even their husbands' older male relatives. They bring dowries with them, but otherwise do not usually share with their

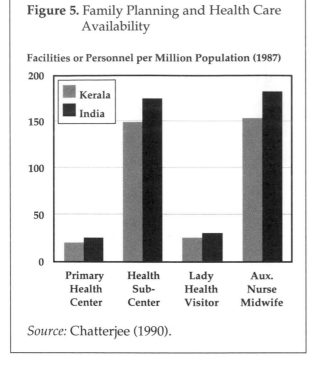

Figure 5. Family Planning and Health Care Availability

Facilities or Personnel per Million Population (1987)

Legend: Kerala, India

Categories: Primary Health Center, Health Sub-Center, Lady Health Visitor, Aux. Nurse Midwife

Source: Chatterjee (1990).

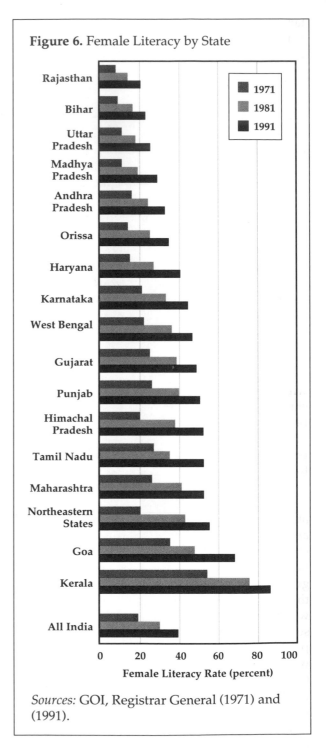

Figure 6. Female Literacy by State

Legend: 1971, 1981, 1991

States: Rajasthan, Bihar, Uttar Pradesh, Madhya Pradesh, Andhra Pradesh, Orissa, Haryana, Karnataka, West Bengal, Gujarat, Punjab, Himachal Pradesh, Tamil Nadu, Maharashtra, Northeastern States, Goa, Kerala, All India

Female Literacy Rate (percent)

Sources: GOI, Registrar General (1971) and (1991).

own brothers in the inheritance of family land and other assets. Depending on caste and class, women's work opportunities are restricted by convention and labor market segmentation. Typically, in rural areas women and girls of landholding households work primarily in unpaid agricultural and household tasks, which bring little economic independence (Basu, 3–4). In poor families, daughters are often regarded as an economic burden, while on sons are laid all hopes for family advancement and security. Such attitudes underlie the unequal treatment that leads to girls' poorer survival probabilities and school attendance. Girls are far more likely to be taken out of school to help with household chores or to care for a younger sibling. Thus, in most rural areas of North India, female literacy rates remain well below thirty percent (Srinivasan, Table 27). *(See Figure 6.)*

In Kerala, by contrast, at the southern tip of India, women historically enjoyed high status as artists, philosophers, and poets. A matrilineal and matrilocal tradition had by the 11th century developed into a widespread system of inheritance through the female line, giving women an inde-

pendent outlook and social influence. In the upper classes, women were educated along with boys, not only in arts and letters but also in military skills. In fact, one of the queens of South Travancore had as her personal bodyguard a troop of 500 soldiers—all women (Nayar, 218).

This tradition of influence and independence has led to a far more equal role for women in Keralan society. As early as 1901, in part due to the efforts of Christian missionaries, Travancore had the highest female literacy rate in India, and the average age at which women married exceeded 17—a figure still not equalled in several northern Indian states. In 1917, the female ruler of Travancore introduced free and compulsory education for all children and opened primary schools in every village. By 1935, another female ruler of Travancore, in a presidential address to the All India Women's conference, could state with some satisfaction: "The woman is here recognized as the head of the family and succession is traced through her. No restriction on the holding or disposal of property and no inequalities regarding education, social life, or cultural growth have hampered our sex. Not only has our history afforded instances of queens who have stamped their individuality on the chronicles of their country but in the fine arts and philosophy women have played a notable part. The equality of women with men in the matter of political and property rights is today an established fact" (Nayar, 218).

After Independence the state government initiated a large-scale effort to extend basic education and health services to women from backward communities, and founded professional institutions open to women at the undergraduate and graduate levels. As a consequence, by the time the *Second India Study* was undertaken, not only were females equally represented as students at secondary and post-secondary levels, over forty percent of the high school and college *teachers* were women. Women also make up a large fraction of other professions, including medicine and public administration. By 1971, 35 percent of economically active women in Kerala worked outside of agriculture, compared to only 20 percent in India as a whole (Nayar, 212–216).

Today, the literacy rate of Keralan women approaches 90 percent, the fertility rate is below re-

placement level, over 70 percent of deliveries take place in an equipped health facility, and the infant mortality rate is as low as New York City's (GOI, 1991 Census). While the family planning service statistics substantially overstate the use of contraceptives in many north Indian states, they greatly understate the prevalence of contraceptive use in Kerala because many women rely on private providers rather than on government clinics.

Clearly, the differences in contraceptive usage among Keralan and Indian women in North India—to say nothing of differences in average marriage age—are far too great to be explained by regional differences in access to services.

Kerala's experience deepens our understanding of the link between development and the demographic transition. It has become fashionable to claim that "contraceptives are the best contraceptive," implying that providing high quality family planning services is the best way to reduce fertility. Proponents of this view point to the close correlation between contraceptive usage and fertility decline around the world, but fail to ask *why* women in some societies contracept effectively while others elsewhere do not. Clearly, the differences in contraceptive usage among Keralan and Indian women in North India—to say nothing of differences in average marriage age—are far too great to be explained by regional differences in access to services. Such differences exist, even in a nationally funded and organized program, but explain little or none of the wide regional differences in marital fertility and contraceptive usage in India (Srinivasan, Tables 28–30). Social and cultural variables matter. In fact, differences in fertility rates among Indian states are far less closely correlated with any measure of family planning service availability than they are with the distance of the state's capital from the Khyber Pass, the traditional invasion route into the Indian sub-

19

continent from Western Asia. *(See Figure 7.)*

Others point to differences in female literacy as the key, and such differences do indeed correlate highly with differences in both fertility and infant mortality. But, female literacy is itself only an indicator of a more fundamental societal orientation that encourages and supports the education of women, and provides the social and economic opportunities that justify an investment in women's schooling. The Keralan experience, contrasted with continuing high fertility in more gender-biassed parts of India, reinforces the conclusion that development is closely linked to demographic transition, but equates development not merely with increases in economic output, but with social transformations that afford women greater autonomy, influence, and opportunities for self-determination.

India's experience since the *Second India Study* supports a middle position, to which a growing majority of social scientists and policy-makers subscribe. It holds that *both* services *and* development are important in the demographic transition. India's expanding network of primary health centers and family planning clinics, its food distribution and nutrition interventions, its immunization and communicable disease control programs, and its investments in schooling and safe water supplies have helped lower mortality rates beneath those typical of countries at comparable income levels. But poverty, illiteracy, malnutrition, and unhealthy living conditions keep death rates in many parts of India far above those in more-developed countries. Similarly, although the Government of India has sustained a massive family planning program, which has contributed to the fertility decline, the slow pace of economic development during the 1970s retarded the pace of demographic change, and the growing differences in birth rates among India's regions demonstrate the importance of modernization and social equity.

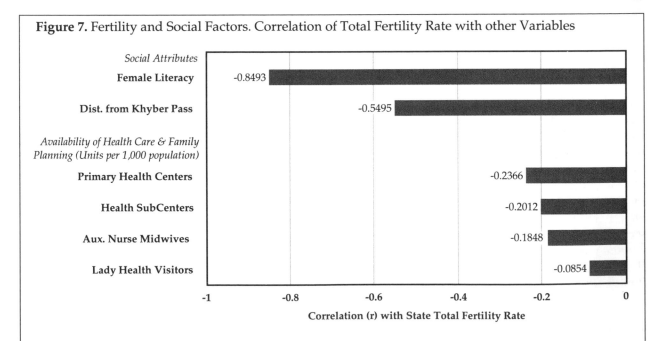

Figure 7. Fertility and Social Factors. Correlation of Total Fertility Rate with other Variables

Social Attributes
Female Literacy -0.8493
Dist. from Khyber Pass -0.5495

Availability of Health Care & Family Planning (Units per 1,000 population)
Primary Health Centers -0.2366
Health SubCenters -0.2012
Aux. Nurse Midwives -0.1848
Lady Health Visitors -0.0854

Correlation (r) with State Total Fertility Rate

Note: State-wise data exclude Jammu and Kashmir.
Sources: Health and Family Planning Data (1987) from Chatterjee (1990). Female Literacy (1988) and TFR (1989) from Srinivasan (1993).

III. Macroeconomic Developments, Employment, and Poverty

"This, then, is the cruel and self-perpetuating dilemma that governments face in underdeveloped countries overburdened for long periods with high birth rates: their plans for progress evaporate into massive efforts merely to maintain the status quo."

    Robert McNamara, President of the World Bank Group, in an address at the University of Notre Dame, 1969

Overall economic growth in India accelerated from about 3.5 percent per year in the 1970s to well over 5 percent in the 1980s. Given that population growth held steady at 2.1–2.2 percent annually, near the top of *Second India Study* projections, this acceleration in economic growth in the 1980s more than doubled the pace at which average per capita incomes were rising, compared to the 1970s and earlier decades. Despite little improvement in the distribution of income and sluggish expansion in employment opportunities in agriculture or organized industry, faster improvement in per capita incomes permitted modest reductions in the percentage—and in the absolute number—of Indians living below the poverty line. Nonetheless, even in 1990–91, India remained a poverty stricken country, with almost 40 percent of its citizens unable to afford a nutritionally adequate diet.

A. Growth and Structural Change

The *Second India Study* of the economy considered four economic scenarios, based on average GDP growth rates of 3, 5, 7 and 9 percent per year

through the end of the century. Each scenario assumed gradually accelerating growth. The 5-percent scenario postulated an acceleration from the three decades long rate of growth of 3.5 percent p.a. to 3.9 percent in the later 1970s, 5.1 percent in the second half of the 1980s and 6.3 percent in the second half of the 1990s. In fact, GDP growth in the later 1970s was only 3.7 percent, but growth accelerated rapidly to 6.1 percent in the second half of the 1980s, midway between the *Second India's* 5 and 7 percent growth paths. India's economic growth performance over this period, though widely criticized at home and abroad, was actually faster than that of OECD countries as a group. It suffered by comparison only to its own targets and to the performance of other Asian countries, many of which sustained much faster growth over the period. By 1990–91, India's GDP was slightly larger than had been projected under the 5-percent growth scenario. However, since 1990–91, after sharp contractionary policies were adopted to counter excessive internal and external deficits, growth has fallen back to an average of about 3 to 4 percent per year. It remains to be seen whether comprehensive economic policy reforms adopted during the early 1990s will regain the high growth rates of the late 1980s.

Structural changes in the economy have been close to those implied by the *Second India Study*'s 5-percent scenario. Since India is a large economy in which foreign trade plays a relatively small role, the structure of production is determined largely by internal demand. As per capita incomes rise, agriculture's share in total expenditure goes down. The *Second India Study* foresaw that, with 5 percent growth, the share of agriculture in GDP would fall rapidly, from 46 percent in 1973–74 to 35 percent in 1990–91; the secondary sector (mining, manufacturing, public utilities and construction) would increase its share from 22 to 29 percent, and the tertiary (service) sector from 32 to 36 percent. These projections have turned out to be very close to the mark. *(See Figure 8.)*

The dominant economic model of the 1950s and 1960s presumed that the large pools of unproductive workers found in agriculture would gradually be reduced by rapid growth in other sectors. However, in those decades GDP grew too slowly to provide alternative livelihoods for India's rural laborers. Agriculture's share of the

labor force remained over 70 percent in 1970, and the average value added per worker in agriculture had fallen to only 27 percent of that in the rest of the economy—one reason why rural poverty remained so widespread. Even in the 1980s, though non-agricultural output has grown more rapidly than it had before, those economic sectors have not generated many jobs, so agriculture's share in the labor force was still nearly 65 percent in 1987–88, the last year for which the National Sample Survey provided labor force data, and value added per agricultural worker was on average less than one quarter of that in other sectors. Although the expected transition from employment in agriculture to other sectors seems under way, value added per agricultural worker has not yet started to climb relative to levels in other sectors of the economy. So, sectoral disparities in output per worker are still large.

So are regional disparities. The richest states have improved their absolute and relative position over the past 20 years, not at the expense of the poorest ones but of those in the middle. In 1970–71, the four northwestern states of Maharashtra, Gujarat, Haryana, and Punjab surpassed the national average income by at least 30 percent. Except for Gujarat, they improved their relative position still further in the next two decades. By 1988–89, Punjab, the richest state, had an average income 85 percent above that of the nation. Favorably endowed to begin with, the Punjab and Haryana, along with well irrigated regions of other states, have been the main beneficiaries of agricultural policies and of the Green Revolution.

In Bihar, the poorest state, incomes in 1970–71 were only two thirds of the all-India average. Next on the ladder up, at about 80 percent, were the contiguous states of Uttar Pradesh, Madhya Pradesh, and Orissa. During the 1970s and 1980s, none of these states improved their relative position appreciably. They were able to keep up with the average growth in Indian per capita incomes, but continued to be the center of India's poverty belt in Eastern India.

The next group of states, with per capita incomes near India's average in 1970–71, consisted

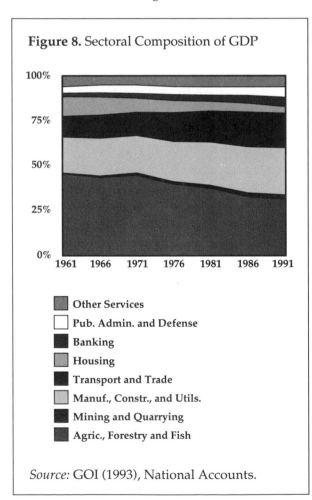

Figure 8. Sectoral Composition of GDP

- Other Services
- Pub. Admin. and Defense
- Banking
- Housing
- Transport and Trade
- Manuf., Constr., and Utils.
- Mining and Quarrying
- Agric., Forestry and Fish

Source: GOI (1993), National Accounts.

of Rajasthan, Andhra Pradesh, Kerala, Tamil Nadu, and Karnataka. Among those, Rajasthan and Kerala slipped back by about ten percentage points of average income over the two decades. More serious was the relative loss for West Bengal: it fell from about 120 to 100 percent of the nationwide average. These states are located widely apart, and there appears to be no common reason for their relative lag in income growth. Kerala's apparent lag is somewhat misleading since its well-educated and mobile population supplemented domestic production with significant earnings and remittances from the Middle East and elsewhere, earnings that are not included in gross domestic product.

For several years the United Nations Development Programme has published the Human Development Indicator (HDI), an index of per capita real income, life expectancy and adult literacy. In terms of this indicator, India as a nation is comparable to Tanzania, Pakistan, Madagascar and Papua New Guinea. Indian states' ranking on the HDI is similar to their ranking by per capita income, with two important exceptions: Kerala ranks 11th out of 16 major states in income, but first on the Human Development Index because life expectancy and literacy are so high. Uttar Pradesh, the largest state, is 12th in per capita income and last in terms of human development.

Price movements also affected income distribution and poverty trends. Urban costs of living rose substantially relative to those in rural areas. The average gap between rural and urban price levels for the basket of goods relevant to households at the poverty line widened from 15 percent in 1973–74 to 43 percent by 1987–88. Since the urban poor must purchase almost all of their necessities, oftentimes even water, and have few opportunities to gather resources from the commons, these adverse price movements can cause real hardships and indeed exacerbated urban poverty. In addition, prices varied substantially from one rural area to another: the cost of living at the poverty line in rural Andhra Pradesh in 1987–88, for example, was only 70 percent of the cost of living in rural West Bengal and Kerala and half of the cost of living in Bombay.

In the 1970s, as the result of all these forces, the income distribution among households became somewhat more unequal. Between 1973–74 and 1977–78, for example, when successive rounds of the National Sample Survey were implemented, the share of the upper three deciles in the expenditure distribution increased from 49.6 to 51.7 percent in rural areas and from 51.7 to 55.7 percent in urban areas. The share of the poorest three deciles declined from 15.7 to 14.9 percent and from 15.1 to 13.2 percent in rural and urban areas, respectively. In the next decade, the distribution of expenditures across households changed little.

B. Labor Force, Employment, and Wages

While India's population growth rate has been steady over the last three decades, falling fertility and mortality rates decreased the percentage of young people (not yet 15) in the population and raised that of the elderly (over 60). The working age population (15 to 59) increased from 52 to 55 percent between 1971 and 1991. Nonetheless, the overall labor participation rate remained virtually unchanged at 41 to 42 percent of the total population, implying that the percentage of working age people actually working has decreased. One explanation is that a larger proportion of young people are continuing their education. Another is that even though female participation rates are rising in rural and urban areas, they are so much lower in urban areas that the shift to an increasingly urban population has reduced female labor force participation rates overall. Participation rates are 54 and 50 percent, respectively, for rural and urban males, and 34 and 14 percent for rural and urban females. In much of India, it remains more acceptable for females to work on their household farms or in family activities than outside the home.

Nonetheless, as the *Second India Study* had foreseen, between 1971 and 1991 the labor force increased by 123 million, growing faster than the total population. In the 1980s alone, it increased from some 290 to 350 million, which is 22 percent higher than the *Second India Study* projected. The employment problem turned out to be even more intractable than the *Second India Study* had anticipated.

In a country in which few households have assets from which they can derive an income and government welfare programs are so limited, several members of each household must work if it is to escape destitution. Since most people cannot afford to be unemployed for long, low unemployment figures aren't by themselves necessarily a positive sign. Because the educated vie for formal employment, can afford to wait for a job, and are also much more likely to register as unemployed while waiting, they form a disproportionate share (40 percent) of the officially unemployed. However, 90 percent of India's labor force works in the informal sector, which includes agricultural labor, most transportation, trade, small-scale, and cottage industries, and services. These easy-to-enter livelihoods are the last resort for many people, so underemployment is widespread and productivity is low. Millions of people work long hours for miserable returns.

Because growth was slow until the 1980s and the capital-labor ratio rose throughout the organized sectors of the economy and agriculture, formal employment opportunities failed to increase sufficiently to absorb new labor force entrants and cut into the enormous residue of underemployment in informal activities. The economy seemed to be playing out the worst-case scenario depicted by the *Second India Study*. After the national election of 1972, development policy shifted dramatically to attack poverty and underemployment directly through publicly-funded employment creation and anti-poverty programs, rather than relying on overall economic development.

Three types of approaches have been used to help the poor, apart from traditional efforts in education, health, and family planning, in which public expenditures have not been targeted particularly to the needs of low income households. The first is to provide the poor with basic necessities (mainly food) at low, subsidized prices. The second is to provide them with additional wage employment. The third is to help them acquire income-producing assets, such as milk cows or bullock carts.

In the first category, the Public Distribution System is the most important program, providing mainly foodgrains at subsidized prices. Over time, program costs have escalated, recently amounting to about 0.5 percent of GDP. The system has covered urban areas; in only a few states has it been effective in the countryside. Subsidized sales have unfortunately not been well targeted to the poor; rather, a broad spectrum of low and middle class households participate in subsidized purchases, and substantial quantities of foodgrains leak into the open market. Although it is flawed as an anti-poverty instrument, the system has undoubtedly been an important link in a safety net for the poor.

Through the National Rural Employment Program and the Rural Landless Employment Guarantee Program, the government has provided supplemental wage employment. By the late 1980s, annual expenditures on these two programs together totalled some Rs. 13 billion, or close to 0.3 percent of GNP, and generated more than 500 million person days of employment per year. Still, this was equivalent to only 0.6 percent of overall rural employment—important to many poor households, but an insignificant part of the total labor market.

One state, Maharashtra, has run a different and much larger employment program. Under its 1977 Employment Guarantee Act, each worker presenting himself or herself for work is guaranteed employment, with no limit set by annual budgetary allocations. Daily attendance in the mid-1980s has averaged over 3.5 percent of total daily rural employment in the state, and 12 percent of employment of the poor. In some districts and periods, the participation rate has ranged much higher. Without spending limits, the program costs grew to exceed 10 percent of the state's development budget, and 1 percent of state GDP. By offering wages below prevailing market rates, the program automatically targeted itself to poor households.

The third major poverty alleviation program is the Integrated Rural Development Program, which provides bank loans—subsidized by 25–50 percent by central and state governments—to stimulate rural self-employment by helping people acquire income-producing assets. Investments made under this program have recently amounted to about 0.4 percent of GDP. Generally, no single client receives more than a few thousand Rupees to invest, so it has been possible to spread funds widely—to about 27 million households between 1980 and 1988. A large majority of the beneficiaries (some of whom received a second dose of assistance) were poor, and 35 percent belonged to scheduled castes or tribes. This program has also suffered from lapses in targeting, and results have been mixed: many beneficiaries have not been able to hold on to their assets, and others have derived little income from theirs.

Collectively, the various direct anti-poverty programs have probably helped curtail or reduce poverty. But even programs that require large financial and administrative resources cannot make up for structural failures in economic development. Faster growth over the 1980s has undoubtedly done more to reduce poverty.

Growth accelerated to 5 percent per year in the first half of the 1980s and to 6 percent in the second half. *(See Figure 9.)* Yet, employment data give a mixed picture. Overall employment growth between 1983 and 1987–88 lagged behind labor force growth, employment growth in manufacturing decelerated, especially in large establishments, and whatever little formal employment growth there was came from the public sector. On-farm agricultural employment grew slowly, even in the northwestern states where

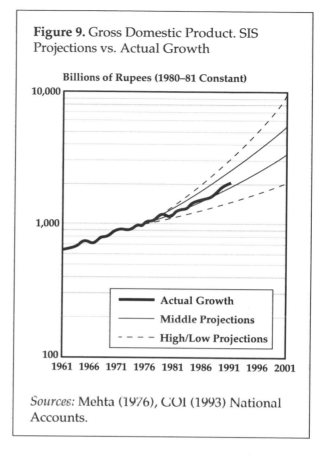

Figure 9. Gross Domestic Product. SIS Projections vs. Actual Growth

Billions of Rupees (1980–81 Constant)

Sources: Mehta (1976), COI (1993) National Accounts.

output was buoyant. On the other hand, non-agricultural rural employment seemed to have expanded more rapidly. Significant gains probably occurred as casual workers (mainly male) migrated daily to nearby urban areas—possible because transport links have improved. Increasing personal mobility helped reduce unemployment in slow-growing regions.

By far the most encouraging labor market indicator is the improvement in real wages virtually throughout India since the GDP growth rate started to pick up (Hanson [a] [1990]; Krishnan [1991]). Even in the 1970s, agricultural real wage rates for males rose in all but four states (Punjab, Haryana, Maharashtra and Assam). Between 1980 and 1987, they rose in all major states and quite rapidly in some. Per day worked in Orissa, a man could support 1.9 persons at the poverty level for a day in 1970 and 2.5 people by 1987. In Madhya Pradesh, another poor state, these numbers were

1.8 and 3.2, respectively, and in a better-off state such as Gujarat, 2.8 and 4.5.

Real agricultural wage rates for females moved upward even more consistently. In the 1970s, they declined only in Bihar, and in the 1980s only in Tamil Nadu. The median increase from the early 1970s to the mid 1980s was 2.7 and 1.8 percent per year for females and males, respectively. In 12 out of 15 states, the ratio between female and male wage rates improved, and the median ratio went up from .71 to .82. This change probably reflected the increased need for small farmers to seek off-farm employment and the consequent tendency for their spouses to take over the farm work.

C. Poverty Trends

This evident rise in real wage rates, signalling some tightening of labor markets, is reflected in the data on poverty trends. The most commonly used poverty indicator is simply the percentage of the population below the "poverty line." This measure omits a household's asset and debt position, its access to public and communal resources, and even the extent to which its expenditures fall short of the poverty line. The availability of publicly financed services and of communal resources greatly affects the living standards of low-income households. Fuels, fodder, and a variety of foods and materials gathered from the wild have traditionally met as much as one fourth of the total consumption needs in low-income households. All over India, such communal resources have become scarcer, as a later chapter details, but in some regions the situation is far more acute than in others. Since consumption and expenditure surveys don't capture diminished availability of such gathered resources perfectly, they understate the vulnerability of the rural poor and overstate any improvement in welfare.

Every five years, the National Sample Survey collects extensive data in the urban and rural areas of each state on household expenditure patterns. Detailed price data are used to compare expenditures in real terms in different regions and time periods. There are difficulties in assessing

trends, even with this simple measure. For example, the National Sample Surveys apparently miss a significant but varying fraction of total consumption, more of which consists of goods and services purchased by better-off households. Moreover, prices and consumption patterns vary across regions and over time so that a single price index or budgetary allocation cannot capture the diversity of trends very accurately.

Nonetheless, an expert group instituted by the Planning Commission recently reviewed earlier poverty estimates and produced a revised set that the government has adopted. They show steady overall progress in reducing the prevalence of poverty in India, from 55 percent of the population in 1973 to 45 percent a decade later, and to 39 percent in 1987–88, the latest year for which NSS data are available. In view of the continued rapid growth, it is likely that poverty in 1990–91 had become still less widespread. However, because of the population increase during these years, the *number* of people below the poverty line fell by less than 5 percent from 322 to 313 million between 1973 and 1988.

Because of the population increase during these years, the number *of people below the poverty line fell by less than 5 percent from 322 to 313 million between 1973 and 1988.*

Rural and urban poverty trends converged over this period because the rural poverty rate fell almost twice as fast—from 56 to 46 percent between 1973 and 1983 and then to 39 percent by 1988. *(See Figure 10.)* In urban areas, where the poverty rate also declined from 49 percent in 1973 to 42 percent in 1983, it was still at 40 percent in 1988. By the late 1980s, not only had poverty become more prevalent in urban areas: the *number* of poor people in cities had increased by 23 million, almost 40 percent.

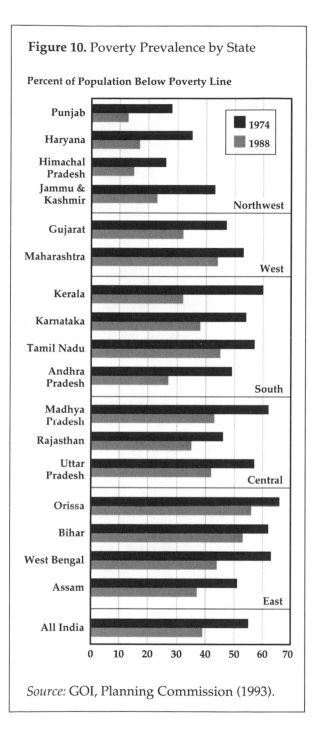

Figure 10. Poverty Prevalence by State

Percent of Population Below Poverty Line

Source: GOI, Planning Commission (1993).

All states experienced substantial reductions in poverty, amounting to at least 9 percentage points over the 15-year period. However, the ranking of states by poverty prevalence remained mostly unchanged. Orissa, Bihar, Tamil Nadu, and West Bengal in Eastern India remained the states most stricken by poverty; Haryana, Punjab in Northwest India, and the hill states of Himachal Pradesh, Jammu and Kashmir, the least so. Kerala and Maharashtra were the only states to change their position substantially. Although Kerala's GDP grew only slowly, remittances and transfers from abroad reduced poverty significantly. Maharashtra, a very diverse state with affluent and very poor regions (and significant urban poverty and inequalities), combines a relatively high average income with a high poverty level. In 1987–88, 44 percent of its population was poor.

D. Reasons Behind the Growth Acceleration

Why did the rate of increase in per capita incomes double during the 1980s after almost three decades of slow growth? Faster growth was *not* the result of any demographic change: the rate of population increase during the 1980s remained almost as high as in the 1970s and just as high as it was in the 1960s. Labor force participation rates remained unchanged. Moreover, the number of people added to the population during the 1980s was greater than in any prior decade.

Increases in productive capacity were significant. During the 1970s and 1980s, investment rates rose from about 17 percent of GDP around 1971 to 26 percent in 1991. Over 90 percent of this growth was financed through domestic savings, increasingly generated through higher savings rates in the private sector. Thus, continued population growth apparently did not have the often feared effect of reducing the household savings rate. Public sector savings, however, declined from about 4 to 2 percent of GDP, and foreign capital inflows financed an almost constant share of investment. Private savings also became more fluid over time. In the early 1970s, about two thirds of household savings were invested in physical assets, such as real estate and gold, and one third in financial assets; over the last two decades this ratio has shifted to fifty-fifty. Intermediation through financial institutions potentially redirected private savings toward investments with higher returns.

Over the 1970s and 1980s, the sectoral allocation of investment has changed in important ways. Agriculture's share declined from 16 to 10.5 percent of total investment, in line with the reduced weight of the sector in GDP. Real estate's share declined from 12 to 9 percent. Public utilities (mainly electricity) went from 9 to 12.5 percent. Transport went from 11 to over 12 percent. Rapid increases in investment in these sectors helped break infrastructural bottlenecks in the economy. Two small but leading sectors also expanded their investment shares rapidly; mining (largely petroleum) went from less than 2 to 6 percent, and banking from 0.5 to 2.5 percent. Expansion in domestic petroleum and gas production helped avert more serious foreign exchange problems after the oil shocks of the 1970s and early 1980s.

Within the public sector, which maintained a constant share in total investment despite its falling savings rate, there were also important reallocations. Of greatest significance, outlays on public sector industry, mostly heavy industries, declined from 23 to 12 percent of total Development Plan outlays, losing out to expenditures on electric power. In view of the low returns and substantial underutilization of capacity in public sector heavy industries, and the serious power shortages during the period that constrained industrial production, this shift undoubtedly contributed to faster growth.

Aside from such increases in the capital stock, other supply side improvements contributed to faster growth in the 1980s. Remittances from Indian workers in the Middle East surged remarkably. Increasing domestic production and falling world oil prices reduced the burden of petroleum imports. Both these developments helped relax foreign exchange shortages. Larger reserve stocks of foodgrains, the greater importance of irrigated crops in overall farm production, and the shrinking share of agriculture in total output made the economy less hostage to unfavorable weather. For these reasons, the government was better able

to avoid cyclical "stop-go" macroeconomic policies to avert inflation or balance of payments problems during the 1980s.

In addition, there were some shifts in the pervasive pattern of government control over the economy to reduce bureaucratic regulation and to increase the private sector's ability to adapt and respond to new opportunities. Such changes included some relaxation of licensing requirements for new investments, and of quantitative restrictions on imports of industrial materials and equipment. In addition, some commodities once subject to price controls and rationing were decontrolled. Tariffs on some industrial materials and intermediates were also cut back, reducing distortions and increasing competition in the economy. From 1980–81 to 1984–85, the average degree of protection against imports in industry fell from 79 to 37 percent of the cif import price. Meanwhile, the rupee also depreciated substantially over the 1980s, making the economy more competitive internationally. These changes presaged the far more comprehensive reforms in economic policy of the 1990s, but in themselves enabled and encouraged the private sector to raise output in response to more buoyant demand growth.

On the demand side, growth was stimulated by an expansionary fiscal policy. Unlike many other developing countries, India had avoided excessive foreign borrowing in the wake of the oil shocks of the 1970s and early 1980s, thanks to rising domestic oil production, remittances from workers in the Middle East, and a traditionally conservative macroeconomic regime. In the 1980s, when other developing countries were desperately retrenching to accommodate capital outflows and suffering deep recessions, India was able to expand. Over the 1980s, government revenues rose by about 5 percent of GDP because of tax rationalization, petroleum revenues, and economic growth, but public expenditures increased even faster, leading to a deficit of 9 percent of GDP. This increase in expenditures consisted mostly of transfers and subsidies to the private sector, which fed an upsurge in domestic demand and translated into faster growth in consumer goods and service industries. This, in turn, stimulated demand for raw materials and intermediates.

India evidently entered the 1980s with significant excess capacity and underutilized productive potential. Therefore, when demand surged and supply constraints were eased, output could increase without a proportionate rise in investment. The incremental capital-output ratio declined, indicating more efficient use of capital. Labor productivity also increased. Enterprises raised production without hiring many new workers. Productivity improvements like these raised value added and reduced production costs as output expanded.

However, increasing fiscal deficits are economically unsustainable. During the world recession in the early 1990s, falling exports, the loss of export markets in the former Soviet Union, and surging imports led to a balance of payments crisis and forced government to retrench. The economy slipped back to slower growth rates. However, the economic reforms begun in the 1980s and broadened and accelerated under a new government have the potential to return the economy to the faster growth path established during the 1980s.

India's overall experience during the 1970s and 1980s illustrates the difficulties of raising living standards substantially as population grows rapidly. Although overly bureaucratic and centralized regulation slowed the economic growth rate, prudent macroeconomic policies enabled India to weather the oil price shocks of the 1970s and the debt crisis of the 1980s. The GDP growth rate in the 1970s was quite respectable by comparison with India's past and with the performance of the vast majority of the world's nations, including those of the OECD. In the 1980s, when growth accelerated, India's economy outperformed all but China's, the booming economies of East and Southeast Asia, and a few others. Nonetheless, between 1970–71 and 1990–91 GDP per capita rose from $240 to only $350 per year, which is about the level of Burkina Faso's and Benin's. At the end of the period, the number of Indians living in absolute poverty still exceeded 300 million, and had declined only by a few percent in two decades. Most of the increased scores of millions in the labor force worked in unproductive, insecure, and low-earning jobs. An enormous development effort still lay ahead.

IV. Food, Agriculture, and Water

"…the green revolution has won a temporary success in man's war against hunger and deprivation: it has given man a breathing space. If fully implemented, the revolution can provide sufficient food for sustenance during the next three decades. But the frightening power of human reproduction must also be curbed; otherwise, the success of the green revolution will be ephemeral only."

Norman Borlaug, Director of the Wheat Research and Production Program at CYMMT, on accepting the Nobel Peace Prize, 1970

India's agricultural performance since 1970 has confounded those who feared a Malthusian spectre of famine, but also those who saw the emerging "Green Revolution" as a technological breakthrough into markedly higher rates of agricultural growth. In fact, between 1970–71 and 1990–91, foodgrains and overall agricultural output kept increasing at the very same long-term trend rates as during the previous 25 years. What the Green Revolution accomplished was to maintain this output growth rate when room for further expansion in the cultivable area was nearly exhausted (Vaidyanathan [a], 23). Per capita food availability improved modestly, in line with the slow improvement in purchasing capacity, but as the 1990s began, a substantial fraction of the population still lacked a nutritionally adequate diet. Moreover, the unmistakably rising resource costs of agricultural production fostered doubts about whether the growth trend could be accelerated to meet demands generated by more rapidly rising incomes. (Vaidyanathan [a], 57).

The *Second India Study* unambiguously rejected the Malthusian idea that the second India would be unable to feed itself. While not unduly euphoric about the recent successes of high-yielding dwarf varieties of wheat and rice—the so-called green revolution—it nonetheless maintained that India's land and water resources, used with demonstrated farming methods of the 1970s, would be sufficient to feed a second, third, and fourth India (Rao [1975], 74). It predicted that in the 1970s, increases would come mainly from greater use of high-yielding seeds, fertilizers, and other inputs in the irrigated areas where initial successes were achieved. Thereafter, yield increases would have to come from extending adaptive research to other crops and agronomic conditions and from establishing the rural institutions and infrastructure needed to spur agricultural development in lagging regions (Rao [1975], 71–84).

The *Second India Study* warned, however, that "increased production of food would provide only a necessary precondition to move towards removal of hunger; the lasting solution to the problem would remain contingent on the removal of poverty, in the sense of enabling the poor to earn the requisites of a decent living in the normal course of working of the economy" (Rao [1975], 3). Rural livelihoods were identified as the key link between raising food output and ensuring adequate purchasing capacity among India's poor:

"Above all, India's success in bringing about increases in agricultural production

31

along with reducing poverty and 'latent hunger' would depend critically on her capacity to carry out basic reforms in the structure of ownership and cultivation of land, to tilt the balance in favor of the small cultivator, tenant, and laborer. With these reforms she would find it possible to face not merely the food problem but also the far more formidable problem of providing livelihood in agriculture to the growing labor force which, for many decades to come, is not expected to move out in sufficient numbers to non-agricultural sectors. Without them, India will have to look for miracles to help her tackle the problems of food and employment for the rural masses" (Rao [1975], 83).

One *Second India Study* scenario of rapid population growth and moderate economic growth did approximate actual trends over the 1970s and 1980s. Nonetheless, the *Second India Study* overestimated the growth of food demand. *(See Figure 11.)* Because cereals and pulses make up such a large part of the low-income household's diet and of India's agricultural acreage, the *Second India Study's* analysis of agricultural production focussed mainly on these foodgrains. With stable prices, no net imports, substantial subsidized distribution to needy households, and sizable additions to stocks, 176 million tons of domestic foodgrains production met actual demand in 1990–91 (Bowonder, *Food*, 24). This represented a 97 percent increase over 1964–65, compared to a projected rise of 115–126 percent (Rao [1975], 53).

Changes in consumption patterns account for most of this overestimate. In both rural and urban areas and at high and low levels of income, households spent more of their available funds on non-food items as the years went by (Vaidyanathan [a], 50). They spent a larger fraction of their food budget on vegetables, oils, dairy products, and other relatively expensive foodstuffs, and commensurately less on foodgrains. Similarly, more was spent on "superior" cereals—rice and wheat—and less on sorghum, millets, and other coarse grains (Radhakrishna & Ravi [1990], cited in Vaidyanathan [a], 50; Vaidyanathan [a], Tables 37–39).

Figure 11. Foodgrains

Total Foodgrains (Millions of Tons)

Sources: Projected Requirements—Rao (1976), *Actual Production*—Bowonder (1993).

This could be the consequence of rising living standards and a greater food availability, which allows a more varied and appealing diet. It also undoubtedly reflects a change in tastes and consumption habits encouraged by increased mobility and improved communications. What is remarkable, however, is that this shift also took place among households at or below the poverty line: those with barely enough resources to obtain the minimum required calories (Bhattacharya [1985], cited in Vaidyanathan [a], 51). *(See Figure 12.)* Even households with inadequate calorie intake did not use additional income to purchase adequate calories in the form of foodgrains, the cheapest available source. The caloric intake of households in the lower third of the expenditure scale hardly improved. *(See Figure 13.)* In fact, the percentage of households whose total monthly expenditures would have allowed them to purchase enough calories, but who nonetheless did not do so, rose substantially over the period, from

Figure 12. Consumption Patterns of the "Very Poor." Budget Shares Allocated to Different Food Types and Non-food

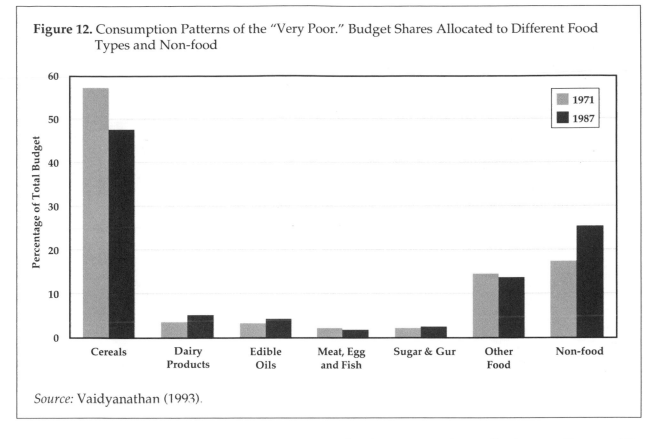

Source: Vaidyanathan (1993).

12 percent in 1977–78 to 37 percent a decade later (GOI, Report of the Expert Group, 62–64).

This strange phenomenon runs counter to normal responses to income and price changes. Part of the explanations may lie in changes in the way households earn and spend money. In both urban and rural areas, the fraction of primary earners who worked as wage laborers has risen substantially. In the villages, as the average farm size has diminished, more people have had to seek off-season or full-time work as day laborers in neighboring villages or nearby towns. People who work away from home eat out and buy other items more often than those working on their own holding (Vaidyanathan [a], 44).

Another explanation may lie in the differing expenditure choices that Indian men and women make. In poor households in which both men and women earn, women spend virtually all the money within their control on maintaining the family; men spend a smaller fraction (Bennett, 15). The fraction of men working for wages has increased much faster than that of women. In rural areas, as men have gone off in search of supplementary or full-time employment, women have taken over more of the work on the family holding. In the prosperous Northwest and the less prosperous East, where gender bias is strong, women are less likely to work outside the household as wage laborers as their family fortunes improve. Working within the household is socially more acceptable. Men are probably receiving a rising share of money earnings and controlling a growing percentage of household expenditures. This may help explain why households are spending less of their combined incomes on basic foods.

A. Change in Nutritional Status

Massive government sales of subsidized foods through 400,000 "fair price shops" has probably

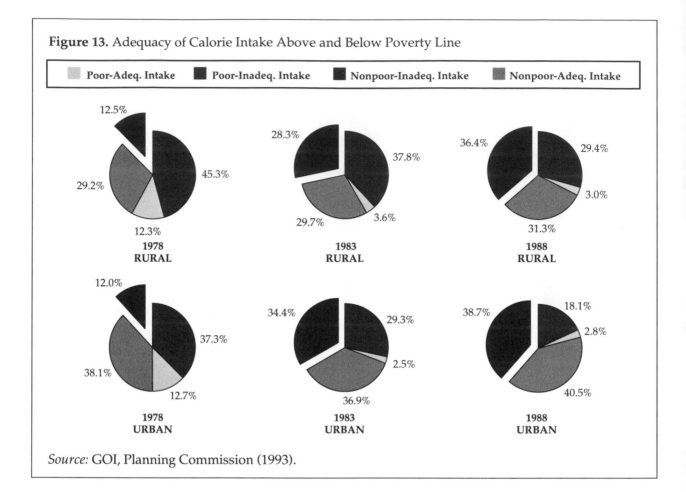

Figure 13. Adequacy of Calorie Intake Above and Below Poverty Line

Poor-Adeq. Intake   Poor-Inadeq. Intake   Nonpoor-Inadeq. Intake   Nonpoor-Adeq. Intake

1978 RURAL — 12.5%, 45.3%, 12.3%, 29.2%

1983 RURAL — 28.3%, 37.8%, 3.6%, 29.7%

1988 RURAL — 36.4%, 29.4%, 3.0%, 31.3%

1978 URBAN — 12.0%, 37.3%, 12.7%, 38.1%

1983 URBAN — 34.4%, 29.3%, 2.5%, 36.9%

1988 URBAN — 38.7%, 18.1%, 2.8%, 40.5%

Source: GOI, Planning Commission (1993).

not changed the nutritional situation very much. Public distribution continues to account for about 12 percent of total availability, and the subsidy has grown significantly from 0.042% of GDP (Rs. 180 million) in 1970–71 to 0.5% of GDP (Rs. 24,500 million) in 1990–91. However, distribution is not closely targeted to the neediest. In fact, the poorest 40 percent of households consume less than half of the subsidized food. Moreover, during the 1980s, distributions were made from supplies procured domestically, and thus didn't add to total availability. On the contrary, domestic procurement of foodgrains exceeded subsidized sales and as a consequence government stocks increased by more than 15 million tons (Vaidyanathan [a], 52–57).

Consequently, much of India's population remains poorly fed. Per capita availability of food-

grains rose by only 6 to 7 percent between the early 1970s and late 1980s, although that of nonstaple food items increased more rapidly. Overall calorie availability from all foods also rose only very modestly. According to available survey information, which is far from conclusive, the percentage of households with adequate protein and calorie intake increased between 1975 and 1989 in some states (including Gujarat, Madhya Pradesh and Orissa) but fell on average slightly in the eight large states surveyed (Bowonder, *Food*, Tables 13–14). *(See Figure 14.)*

Among children under five, an especially vulnerable group, the percentage suffering from severe or moderate undernutrition fell from 72 to 60 percent, according to survey data (UNICEF, Table 2.16). This improvement in a still unsatisfactory situation probably stemmed from lower

Figure 14. Calorie and Protein Intake. Adequacy in Selected States

Percentage of Households with Adequate Protein and Calories

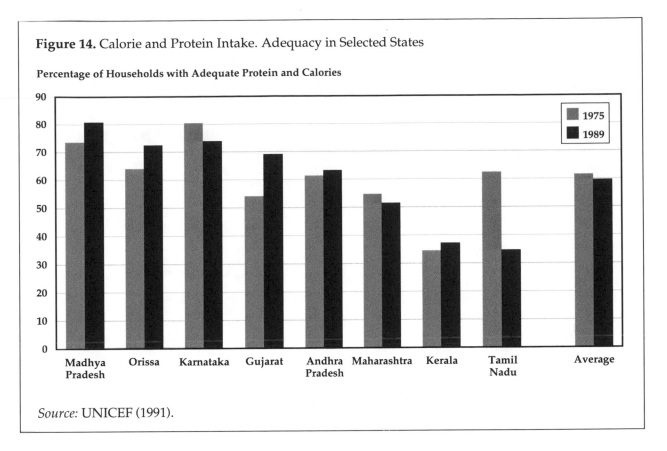

Source: UNICEF (1991).

birth rates, increased access to post-natal care and child health services, nutritional interventions through several public health and food distribution programs, and, especially, advances in the educational status of young mothers. Nutritional deficiencies in young children often stem from repeated bouts of diarrhea and respiratory infections, which impair their ability to absorb food even when they eat enough, so improvements in children's health care—especially by their mothers—is critical (UNICEF, 29–30).

B. Agricultural Production

The overall growth rate between 1970–71 and 1990–91—2.5 percent per year for foodgrains and 2.7 percent for all crops together—masks significant differences among crops, among regions, among seasons, and between irrigated and unirrigated areas (Vaidyanathan [a], 23, 33). It is widely held that population growth acts as a spur to

The Green Revolution has often been called a wheat revolution; it might also be called a tubewell revolution.

agricultural intensification. However, interregional differences in the growth of agricultural production had little to do with differences in population densities or population growth rates, and much to do with differentials in the pace of irrigation development (Vaidyanathan [a], 24). The Green Revolution has often been called a wheat revolution; it might also be called a tubewell revolution. Crops grown in the post-monsoon or winter ("rabi") season have increased rapidly in acreage, yield, and production using irrigation water drawn mainly from wells by farmer-owned and operated pumps. Foremost among these winter crops is wheat. Its acreage increased substantially as a percentage of the total area irrigated. Production grew at 4.9 percent annually and more than doubled over twenty years. High-yielding dwarf wheat varieties, which respond well to fertilizers with adequate moisture control, spread rapidly from 6 million hectares in 1970 to 20 million hectares (87 percent of total wheat acreage, virtually all of it irrigated). Production of rapeseed, mustard and other oilseeds, also mainly winter crops, nearly doubled. (Vaidyanathan [a], 30–33).

Production of "kharif" crops (those dependent on monsoon rains) increased only about half as fast as winter crops. Rice production, although also benefitting from new high-yielding dwarf seed varieties, grew by only 2.8 percent between 1970–71 and 1990–91. Paddy is grown mostly during the monsoons, and more than half of all rice acreage is unirrigated. Moisture control, including drainage of excess water, is difficult in many of the traditional rice-growing areas. There, most of the plots are very small, tenancy is common, rains can be erratic, and canal irrigation is unreliable. Rice production also grew fastest in the tubewell irrigated areas, where drainage problems are few and moisture control is superior. Commercial crops, such as sugarcane and cotton, also did well under irrigation (Vaidyanathan [a], 32). *(See Figure 15.)*

At the other extreme, pulses and such coarse grains as chickpeas and millets have shrunk in acreage and their production has stagnated (Vaidyanathan [a], 14). These staple foodgrains of the poor are usually grown on unirrigated plots, and little varietal improvement has been accomplished. For both these reasons, heavy fertilization offers scant returns and substantial risks, even though most soils are heavily eroded and seriously deficient in nutrients. Yields increased by less than 10 percent over the entire 20-year period, making them relatively unappealing crops for farmers with other opportunities. Dryland regions where these crops are prevalent typically lagged farther behind the regions where groundwater resources could be developed. Techniques

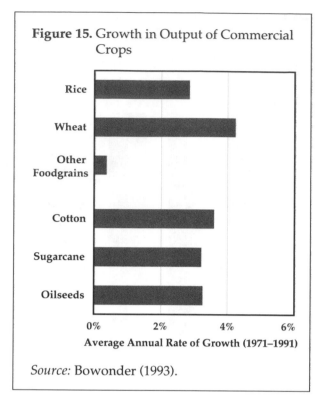

Figure 15. Growth in Output of Commercial Crops

Source: Bowonder (1993).

for conserving moisture, reducing erosion, building soil fertility, and raising yields and farm incomes in dryland areas are known, but they have not been profitable enough to induce widespread investments by individual farmers. Getting farmers in a watershed to cooperate, as many of the techniques require, has proven more difficult than anticipated (Jodha et al., 64). The productivity gains of the green revolution were not extended to dryland agriculture.

During the period, the variability of agricultural production around the trend rate of growth seems to have increased. The exceptions were wheat and sugarcane, two almost entirely irrigated crops. (Ninan & Chandrashekar, A3). For crops grown with less complete moisture control, the sensitivity of yields to rainfall fluctuations has increased as fertilizer use has grown, because the fertilizer response depends so critically on adequate soil moisture. Also, many farmers have shifted away from hardy traditional varieties, defensive crops such as pulses, and inter-cropping, which reduce risk, in favor of higher yielding

> *By the late 1980s, over three quarters of all holdings were less than two hectares in size, and almost three fifths less than one hectare—too small to provide fulltime livelihood or subsistence to an average-sized family.*

crops and varieties. Finally, population pressure has brought sub-marginal lands into production and reduced fallowing (Ninan & Chandrashekar, A2–A7).

C. Agricultural Land Scarcity

As the rural population grew, average farm size fell from 2.3 to 1.7 hectares between 1971 and 1986. By the late 1980s, over three quarters of all holdings were less than two hectares in size, and almost three fifths less than one hectare—too small to provide fulltime livelihood or subsistence to an average-sized family. At the same time, the number and total area in large holdings—over 20 hectares—also diminished (Bowonder, *Food*, 21–23). Total landlessness in rural areas increased only slightly, and the concentration of agricultural land changed little. However, while land *ownership* became slightly less concentrated, operational land *holdings* became somewhat more so. (Vaidyanathan [a], 24) Larger landholders increasingly leased land from smallholders during this period, partly because some smallholdings were uneconomical to operate and partly because large landholders had installed the tubewells that were the key to raising productivity and yields. Thus, despite laws on the books governing tenancy reform and land redistribution, the changes in land tenure that the *Second India Study* identified as critical to rural poverty alleviation did not come about (Vaidyanathan [a], 19–20).

The total area under crops in India has remained nearly constant for the past 20 years. Any new lands brought under the plough just offset areas converted to other uses or lost to soil degradation. For example, about 8.5 million hectares, 6 percent of the cropland base, went out of production because of waterlogging, salinity, or excessive alkalinity. Gullying and erosion took other large areas. The modest 7 percent increase in the gross area cultivated stemmed entirely from increased double-cropping on irrigated farms (Vaidyanathan [a], 23, Table 9).

Bringing more land under cultivation in India would require substantial investments, improved technology, and more favorable economic incentives. For example, 18 million hectares of heavy black soils (vertisols) in central India, more than 10 percent of the gross cropped area, remain fallow during the summer rainy season because they are too hard to cultivate with existing technology. The early rains don't saturate the soil enough to relieve risk of subsequent drought damage to the new plants, and when thoroughly wet the plots are too muddy to cultivate and weed. Neither the available technology nor economic incentives are enough to bring such difficult areas into cultivation (Kampen & Burford, 157–159).

The quality of cropland became increasingly stressed with intensive use. Salinization and alkalinity affect as much as two fifths of India's irrigated soils. Salts build up as mineral-laden water evaporates in the rootzone or on the soil surface, whether drawn up from a high water table through capillary action or deposited on the surface through irrigation. Much of India's farmland has long been deficient in nutrients and organic matter. Organic matter is rapidly oxidized in the heat, leached or eroded away during monsoon rains, or removed through repeated cropping and burning of plant and animal residues. Yet, because of the rural energy deficit, the quantity of organic manures applied in India declined by 20 to 25 percent between 1975 and 1991. The runoff of eroded topsoil into India's rivers and estuaries estimated at around 25 billion tons per year, contains nutrients equivalent to all the chemical fertilizers used in the country. Even though chemical fertilizer use is growing rapidly, micronutrient deficiencies have emerged as important constraints on plant growth in much of India: large percentages of soil samples are deficient in such elements as zinc, iron, and copper (Bowonder, *Environmental Trends*, 6).

These losses in soil fertility have apparently nullified virtually all the yield impact of improvements in seed varieties and agronomic techniques that India's 44 specialized research institutes and 26 state agricultural universities have generated since the early 1970s. Demonstrations of new seeds released for use, grown according to practices recommended by the extension services on farmers' fields have shown no upward trend in yields since 1970–71. *(See Figure 16.)* If anything, trends seem to be pointing downward for all major crops except sorghum ("jowar"). Season-specific and region-specific trend data on demonstration plot yields are needed to confirm this impression. Demonstration plot yields are still far above average yields across India, but it is significant that the yield "envelope" toward which farmers' are progressing has been stagnant or declining despite heavy investments in agricultural research (Vaidyanathan [a], Table 5). Weaknesses in the research that is generated could perhaps explain a slowdown in yield improvements, but a pattern of absolute decline in yields might also indicate deteriorating soil fertility and growing conditions.

For all these reasons, increases in the land resource have not contributed significantly to India's agricultural growth over the past twenty years. Progress in shifting from low- to high-yielding crops has continued. Rapid increases in irrigation, mechanization, and fertilizer use, along with the spread of improved seed varieties have carried the entire burden of raising per hectare yields. But these inputs have grown much faster than output has over the years. *(See Figure 17.)* Total investment in agriculture has been constant in real terms since the early 1970s—maybe even fell slightly in the late 1980s. But this greatly understates total government support for the agricultural sector: in fertilizer plants, rural roads,

rural electrification, and other infrastructure. Over the 20-year period, the number of villages with electricity connections quadrupled, foodgrains storage capacity more than tripled, and the mileage of surfaced roads more than doubled. The volume of institutional agricultural credit outstanding rose from 5 to 9 percent of agricultural gross value added (Vaidyanathan [a], 11–16).

D. Increasing Use of Chemicals

Fertilizer use increased almost six-fold in twenty years, from 2.2 to 12.6 million tons of nutrients. By 1991, fertilizer use per acre in India was no longer low by international standards. In fact, per hectare of agricultural land it was 60 percent *higher* than in the United States, although yields of most major crops are much lower. Moreover, the additional crop output obtained from increases in fertilizer use has declined substantially over the period, even though farmers have become more familiar with chemical fertilizer and improved seed varieties, and despite the spread of irrigation. This may also signal the growing importance of other yield constraints, including deficiencies in micro-nutrients and soil organic matter (Vaidyanathan [a], 29).

There is no longer any difference between large and small farms in their use of chemical fertilizers and improved seed varieties. In this sense, the Green Revolution has thoroughly diffused throughout rural India. The big remaining difference is between irrigated and unirrigated areas. Although the differentials have narrowed since 1970–71, a much higher percentage of irrigated farms use chemical fertilizers, and they apply substantially more nutrients per hectare, so they get much higher yields. However, ecological problems are growing. In the wet rice-growing states of West Bengal, Orissa, Bihar, and Assam, nutrient runoff has encouraged the growth of such aquatic weeds as water hyacinth, which already have infested 40 percent of the total cultivable area.

Pesticide use has increased 3.4 times, growing by more than 6 percent per year between 1970–71

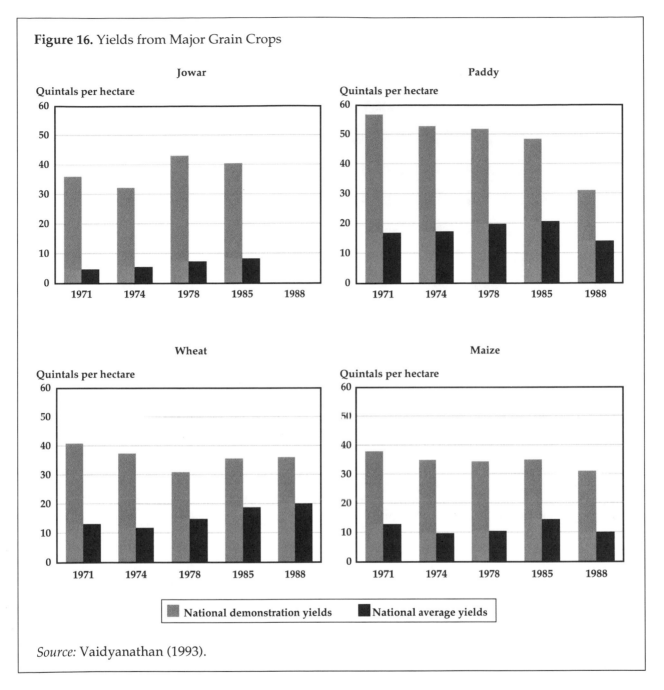

Figure 16. Yields from Major Grain Crops

Jowar

Quintals per hectare

Paddy

Quintals per hectare

Wheat

Quintals per hectare

Maize

Quintals per hectare

☐ National demonstration yields ■ National average yields

Source: Vaidyanathan (1993).

and 1990–91. As cropping intensities increased, as high yielding monocultures have spread, and as farmers' investments in crop production have risen throughout the Green Revolution regions, pest management problems have intensified. Ninety percent of all pesticides are applied in only five states, and more than half are used just on cotton, which occupies only one twentieth of the total cropped area. Indiscriminate pesticide use on such vulnerable crops as cotton have led to pest resistance and the emergence of secondary pests. Consequently, pest management costs have risen above 20 percent of total production costs in some areas (Subba Rao et al., 413). Herbicide-re-

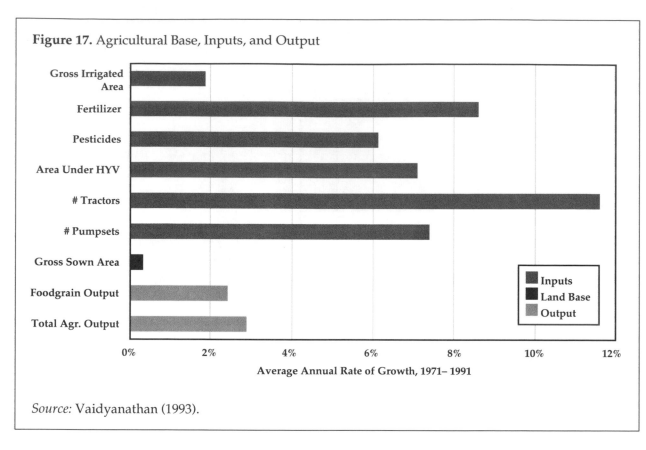

Figure 17. Agricultural Base, Inputs, and Output

Gross Irrigated Area
Fertilizer
Pesticides
Area Under HYV
Tractors
Pumpsets
Gross Sown Area
Foodgrain Output
Total Agr. Output

Inputs
Land Base
Output

0% 2% 4% 6% 8% 10% 12%

Average Annual Rate of Growth, 1971– 1991

Source: Vaidyanathan (1993).

sistant strains of grass weeds emerging where high yielding dwarf wheats are grown seriously threaten future yields (Gianessi & Puffer, 18).

Nearly 70 percent of the pesticides used in India, including DDT, aldrin, methyl parathion, and BHC, are banned or severely restricted on health grounds for agricultural uses in some other countries (Center for Science and the Environment [1985], cited in Joshi & Singh, 97). There are no comprehensive systems for monitoring exposure levels or comprehensive data on health impacts. Yet, local surveys give clear warning signs. In the Punjab, the leading agricultural state, pesticide contamination of food was pervasive in the 1970s, especially in milk and dairy products. Seventy three percent of milk samples from Ludhiana District found excessive DDT residues, averaging five times the legally permitted level. Even mothers' milk contained DDT and BHC residues several times higher than permitted levels. In a Punjabi cotton-growing district, DDT in-

Nearly 70 percent of the pesticides used in India, including DDT, aldrin, methyl parathion, and BHC, are banned or severely restricted on health grounds for agricultural uses in some other countries.

take through mother's milk was 24 times the acceptable daily level. Use of these compounds continues to increase (Dhaliwal & Diliwari, 193–94). Recent findings implicating these estrogen-mimicking compounds in reproductive disorders are grounds for substantial concern (Colburn & Clement, [1992]). More powerful and toxic organophosphates such as methyl parathion have also come into use. Although these substances break down faster and do not accumulate in tissues as DDT does, their use involves both acute and chronic health risks. In a more recent study in an urban market in Rajasthan, 40 percent of vegetable samples were contaminated with organophosphates (Gupta [1990], cited in Joshi and Singh). Since these pesticides may impair the human immune response, they are potentially dangerous to malnourished children subject to repeated infections, since the immune systems of such children are already stressed. This syndrome illustrates the complex linkages among poverty, demographic factors, and the environment.

E. Expansion in Tubewell Irrigation

In most major agricultural states, output per hectare grew by 2 to 4 percent per year in irrigated areas, but showed no significant increase in unirrigated areas. Those districts that achieved rapid growth in output had a much larger fraction of cropped area under irrigation in 1970: they also subsequently increased the area under irrigation more rapidly than other districts did (Vaidyanathan [b], Table 13). Large parts of the Punjab, Haryana, western Uttar Pradesh, and parts of Gujarat, Andhra Pradesh and other alluvial areas with groundwater resources experienced rapid growth. Irrigation was undoubtedly a key factor allowing India's agricultural production to keep pace with the rise in population since the *Second India Study. (See Figure 18.)*

Exploitation of groundwater resources was by far the key irrigation source, except in areas where aquifers are limited. Groundwater irrigation contributed 60 to 70 percent of the increase in net irrigated area between 1970–71 and 1987–88, increasing much more rapidly than either large or small surface irrigation systems (Vaidyanathan [b], Table 5). Over 14 million diesel or electric pumpsets have been installed, supplanting traditional animal or hand-powered lifting devices that can water only a much smaller area. Wells now serve a larger area than the canal systems in which the Central Government has invested so heavily (Vaidyanathan [b], Table 3). Tubewells

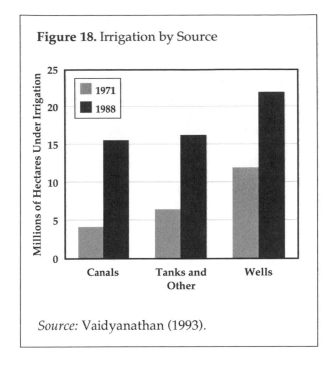

Figure 18. Irrigation by Source

Source: Vaidyanathan (1993).

have also been largely responsible for the double cropping of 18 million additional hectares because they provide a reliable year-round water supply, which many surface systems do not. According to recent estimates, the gross area irrigated by wells is at least 30 million hectares, and possibly much more. Field studies show that in some regions, water sales from well owners to other farmers triple the area irrigated per well, but these additional areas are poorly reflected in statistics.

Even though canal irrigation is heavily subsidized, farmers strongly prefer tubewells. If they can control water supply, they can shift to higher valued crops or high-yielding varieties and use more fertilizer without fear that drought will destroy their investment. Timely water applications markedly increase yields. On average, well owners triple the gross value of output per hectare over rainfed levels, and these farmers have achieved twice the gains in foodgrains yields that canal irrigators have (Shah, 26). Even allowing for higher input costs, well owners have greatly increased their net agricultural incomes.

Although an increasing share of direct public investment in irrigation has gone into the construction of large and medium-sized surface irrigation systems, government strongly supports tubewell irrigation indirectly through loans at subsidized interest rates (many of which are defaulted), favorable pricing of diesel fuel, and—more than anything else—subsidized electricity sales to farmers (Pachauri, 8.4). These subsidies have grown over time. By 1990, tariffs for electrified pumps covered only about one-tenth of energy costs and the aggregate electricity subsidy, much of it attributable to the rural sector, exceeded one percent of GDP.

The benefits have gone primarily to larger farmers, who have increased the use of irrigation most rapidly (Shah, 131). Larger farmers had the money or credit sources to invest in tubewells, and could also utilize pumping capacity more effectively over a larger cropped area. Once in operation, their wells frequently reduced the yield of nearby traditional non-electrified wells, and, in areas where the water table has gone down, put them completely out of operation. Small farmers who couldn't afford to install deeper wells and more powerful pumps were injured. Efforts to control this sort of interference or overuse also erected barriers to entry for later comers. Spacing requirements between wells and restrictions on credit or electricity connections to new wells in regions where groundwater resources were already fully utilized gave an advantage to those who had invested earliest. In effect, those able to put down electrified tubewells gained *de facto* ownership rights over the groundwater resource.

In India, the rights to an immensely valuable resource were distributed *gratis* in a pattern even more unequal than that of land distribution, reinforcing rural inequalities in income and wealth. A potential opportunity to arrange property rights to benefit small farmers and agricultural workers was missed.[1] In addition, agricultural credit, fertilizers, and other inputs that are more productive where water supplies are assured have been subsidized along with electricity. Since well-owners also use these inputs more intensively, they have also benefitted disproportionately from input subsidies. In fact, subsidies of fertilizer, credit, irrigation, and power are distributed dis-

In India, the rights to an immensely valuable resource were distributed **gratis** *in a pattern even more unequal than that of land distribution, reinforcing rural inequalities in income and wealth. A potential opportunity to arrange property rights to benefit small farmers and agricultural workers was missed.*

proportionately in favor of the *more* advanced states, and, within them, to the better-off farmers (Mundle & Rao, 1162).

Nonetheless, tubewell development has benefitted the small farmer and agricultural worker in well-endowed regions as well, though perhaps not as much. The increase in cropping intensity and output that tubewell irrigation made possible has helped keep foodgrain prices down and has provided more work in the fields and in processing industries than would otherwise have been created. For rural households without enough work or production on their own holdings to support themselves, both are important.

In addition, water markets have developed rapidly in some regions, allowing those without wells of their own to share the benefits of groundwater irrigation. Two factors temper well-owners' ability to extract monopoly rents on these water sales. In some regions, potential buyers have more than one potential source. In fact, because holdings are fragmented, many well-owners both buy and sell water on different fields. In addition, because many State Electricity Boards charge only a flat rate per installed horsepower and no energy charge per kwh consumed, making the effective cost of pumping more water virtually zero, well-owners are encouraged to utilize their equipment to the maximum by selling excess water to neighbors (Pachauri, 8.4). While these flat charges have led to an inefficient use of electricity and heavy fiscal losses to the Electricity Boards, they seem to have lowered the price of tubewell water and spread its benefits more widely.

Groundwater irrigation is more sustainable in some regions than in others. In the rainy alluvial areas of eastern India, groundwater resources are underexploited. Plot sizes and landholdings in traditional paddy-growing areas are small, tenancy arrangements are complex, rural electrification has lagged, and the incremental benefits of irrigation are considerably smaller than in semi-arid areas. Without cooperative institutions to share the costs of installing tubewells and the pumped water, farmers have been slow to develop an abundant resource.

In stark contrast, in much of Punjab and Haryana, parts of western Uttar Pradesh, northern and coastal Gujarat, and the alluvial areas in Andhra Pradesh, Tamil Nadu, Gujarat, Orissa, and Kerala, groundwater resources are overexploited. Water tables have been falling by less than a meter to several meters per year (Vaidyanathan [b], 30). Efforts to limit the numbers or spacing of new wells have been inadequate to balanced extraction and recharge. Traditional wells have gone dry, and larger farmers have been forced to extend their wells and enlarge their pumping capacity to manage the higher lifts. Consequently, although masked by flat-rate electricity tariffs and huge subsidies, real pumping costs have risen rapidly, and the resource has been seriously depleted. In extensive coastal areas of Gujarat and Tamil Nadu, the consequences of overexploitation have been even more disastrous. Across millions of hectares, pumping has allowed seawater to infiltrate the aquifer, rendering the water unfit for domestic or agricultural use. Farmers have been trapped in a "prisoner's dilemma": even if they reduced their own extraction, others would continue to pump and they would suffer nonetheless.

At the other extreme, in many areas served by canal irrigation but without adequate drainage, tubewells have prevented the water table from rising and have thereby helped limit problems of waterlogging and salinization. Although surface and groundwater irrigation are not planned or coordinately effectively over a broad area or an entire river basin, individual farmers do adjust their pumping rates to the availability of canal water and rainfall. In these areas, large surface irrigation systems, although inefficient in themselves, have served to recharge the aquifer for tubewells, which, in turn, have served to regulate the water table. Although the *Second India Study* called attention to the need for "conjunctive use" and coordinated planning of groundwater and surface irrigation, what conjunctive use there is has emerged spontaneously through farmers' own investments. For many years, the irrigation authorities even tried to prevent farmers from sinking tubewells within the command areas of surface irrigation systems.

F. Continuing Problems with Canal Irrigation

In contrast to the dynamism evident in farmers' own tubewell investments, large and medium surface irrigation projects, which are entirely the domain of central and state governments, are wrestling without much success with the same problems described by the *Second India Study* twenty years ago. The net area brought under irrigation from these sources has increased by about 3 million hectares since 1970–71, according to Ministry of Agriculture data.[2]

However, the real costs per hectare brought under irrigation have risen, ever more time is needed to complete large irrigation projects, and the apparent gap between the potentially irrigable area and the area actually irrigated has widened. Further, the additional output per hectare achieved by canal irrigation remains far below that achieved by individually controlled tubewells. Economic returns to investments in major and medium surface systems have been disappointingly low (Mishra [1986] and Chambers [1988], cited in Joshi & Singh, 15).

The *Second India Study* foresaw that "...a revolution or quantum jump has to take place in water resources development…—a modernization of concepts, technology and institutions" (Chaturvedi [1976], 73). Prominent among the deficiencies evident in the early 1970s were *ad hoc* decisions about project investments; lengthy "inter-state wranglings" over the allocation of water; a bureaucratic, unprofessional approach to design, planning, and management of large projects; outmoded technologies; poor maintenance; inefficient and inequitable distribution of water and excessive wastage; failure to recover costs; failure to integrate the farmers' interests and constraints into planning and operations; and inattention to ecological considerations, such as disruption of riverine ecology and excessive siltation of reservoirs due to deforestation in upper watersheds (Chaturvedi [1976], 73–77).

The revolution in public sector irrigation management has not taken place. Twenty years later, some problems are more severe. Though strongly linked and potentially complementary, watershed management, groundwater development, irrigation, and agricultural development, are still planned and managed by separate agencies without effective coordination. Social and environmental considerations, including disruption of riverine environments and displacement of communities by construction and flooding, still don't receive enough attention in project planning. Excessive siltation of reservoirs is still shortening the useful lives of irreplaceable storage facilities. In a sample of 12 major dams, a recent study found that actual siltation averages more than twice the designed rate. Another study of five major storage projects found that siltation was curtailing their useful lives by two thirds, on average (Jalees, 246).

As in all countries, there is a large component of "pork barrel" politics in public irrigation programs.

"The political pressures for starting new irrigation projects are very strong: since new projects stand to benefit a large number of farmers, politicians in power view them as instruments for mobilizing electoral support. Large construction projects also happen to be a convenient means for mobilizing

funds for party and other uses. The frequent turnover of both ministers and bureaucratic managers responsible for irrigation further shortens the time horizon of decision making. It militates against strict enforcement of standards of design, efficiency and cost control in projects. Since the consequences of bad decisions or delayed implementation rarely visit the individual minister/officials who make the decision, there is little check on several undesirable tendencies: the propensity to commit the government to new projects without necessary technical preparation and without regard to economic viability, to exert political pressure to get engineers to prepare projects in a hurry and obtain the necessary clearances, and to start far more projects than can be accommodated within the available resources" (Vaidyanathan [b], 21).

Cost recovery has actually deteriorated over the years. Irrigation revenues no longer cover even minimal operation and maintenance—implicitly, a large subsidy to users. According to a recent study, user charges in public irrigation and flood control investments recover only 20 percent of construction and operating costs. This subsidy to favored farmers exceeds 1.5 percent of GDP (Mundle & Rao, Table 4). Not surprisingly, physical facilities (distributories and control structures) are in poor repair—frequently silted up or broken down. Older systems can't meet the needs of more intensive farming, and they require better intermediary storage, flow regulators, and controls. Excessive water seepage and overuse in the head regions has led to serious waterlogging, while farmers at the tail ends of large systems still receive inadequate and unreliable supplies. Underinvestment in drainage has meant that in districts in Haryana, Punjab, and Rajasthan, where the groundwater is too saline for irrigation use, canal irrigation has raised the water table enough to cause soil salinization and drastic reductions in yields. Canal seepage and waterlogging has also contributed to the resurgence of malaria in the irrigated areas, where the resistance of mosquito vectors to DDT and other common insecticides is now widespread (Joshi & Singh, 59).

The *Second India Study* saw the principal remedy for these problems in greater professionalism and particularly in more sophisticated systems engineering and large scale computer modelling of water resource development plans. Now, however, the problem is widely recognized as mainly one of political economy. Funding projects mainly from central government budgetary allocations and distributing water to beneficiaries for far less than its cost or value have politicized the entire allocational process and encouraged what economists call "rent-seeking behavior." Although the problem persists, it is now seen that viable solutions must include a drastic change in incentives and institutional responsibilities. Those affected by projects, whether adversely or favorably, must participate in planning and project decisions.

"Making the whole process more transparent and public is essential. One of the most effective ways to induce more economical use of resources is to give the potential beneficiaries a strong stake—both to be consulted and to participate in the design and operation of each project and also to share a substantial part of the investment cost and/or to meet the full cost of operating and maintaining the facilities" (Vaidyanathan [b], 23).

An expert committee set up by the Planning Committee made recommendations to this effect in 1992.

G. Rural Employment

The more intensive use of irrigation, fertilizers, and high-yielding seed varieties in Indian agriculture over the past 20 years has not generated enough on-farm employment to reduce poverty rapidly among landless agricultural workers and households with inadequate holdings of their own. Although multiple cropping and yields have increased and the overall cropping pattern has shifted toward more labor-using crops, these positive effects on labor demand have been offset by the increasing use of pesticides and herbicides and by mechanization. In Haryana and the Punjab, where output grew fastest, on-farm employment actually fell. In lagging regions, as population grew and the average farm size fell, more and more men and women were pushed off their own farms to seek wage labor elsewhere. Overall, the "employment elasticity," the ratio of the rate of agricultural employment growth to the rate of agricultural output growth, fell continuously over the period, from about 0.7 in the 1970s to 0.5 in the early 1980s, and 0.3 in the late 1980s (Basu & Kashyap, A178). Both casual wage labor and off-farm employment grew substantially as outlets for the rural labor force.

The near stagnation in on-farm employment has been balanced by new opportunities for off-farm work in rural areas and neighboring towns. Increasing mobility and rising incomes have generated employment. Rural works programs and special employment schemes organized and funded by state and central governments have supplemented this market trend. During the 1970s, and increasingly thereafter, India's development strategy has turned toward direct efforts to alleviate poverty by providing employment where needed and creating assets for the benefit of low-income households that didn't have any. During the 1980s, these rural anti-poverty programs were consuming 16 percent of total development outlays, and creating over 350 million man days of work per year (Vaidyanathan [a], 47; Narayana et al., 211). Although the accuracy with which these programs have been targeted on needy populations and the effectiveness with which funds have been spent have been questioned, assessments leave little doubt that the programs have had a significant effect on rural employment and poverty (Vaidyanathan [a], 48). Although the institutional changes that the *Second India Study* foresaw as essential to solve the problem of rural poverty have not come about, a shift in the development strategy toward direct anti-poverty interventions has partially compensated.

Faster overall growth during the 1980s also increased employment opportunities in trade, services, construction, and in towns to which rural households have increasingly migrated for temporary jobs. As noted earlier, casual wage labor off the farm provided an increasing share of rural employment. Together, these opportunities have allowed real wage rates to rise in rural labor markets, despite the growing labor force.

H. Agricultural Price Policies

In some respects, agricultural price policies have added to the rural employment problem that anti-poverty programs were designed to fight. The basic policy during the 1970s and 1980s was to keep foodgrains prices low for the benefit of the urban and rural poor. At various times this has been accomplished through imports, through procurement in surplus states at below market prices, and through distribution at subsidized prices from "fair price" shops (Vaidyanathan [a], 52). Consequently, while some protected agricultural commodities such as sugar and oilseeds have sold well above world market prices, rice and wheat prices have been substantially below world levels. In view of the slow increase in purchasing power and the continuing growth of population, keeping basic food prices low has been a critically important anti-poverty measure.

Indian and foreign experts disagree whether higher foodgrains prices would have resulted in faster agricultural growth, given the technical and institutional constraints on agricultural production. However, to keep low prices from undermining producers' incentives to innovate and adopt advanced practices, modern inputs have been heavily subsidized. Fertilizers, electricity, irrigation, credit, and farm machinery costs have been kept very low. Fertilizer subsidies alone now exceed two thirds of a percent of GDP. Input subsidies totalled roughly 17 percent of agricultural value added during the 1980s, but exceeded 25 and 35 percent of value added, respectively, for the important irrigated crops, wheat and rice (Gulati [1989]). This policy has clearly been successful in stimulating rapid production increases in the regions where tubewell irrigation has developed. While growth in output stimulated employment directly and indirectly, it has had two unintended side effects. First, it has brought

about a massive decline in the *share* of labor in the total input mix in these regions. Other inputs have substituted for labor. While the use of irrigation, machinery, credit, and chemicals has grown substantially faster than output, the use of labor has grown substantially less so. This shift in the pattern of input use, in part a response to price incentives, has limited the growth of on-farm employment.

Second, price policy has worked to the relative disadvantage of dryland agriculture and the regions in which irrigation is unavailable. In 1972–73, the percentage of households below the poverty line was 68 percent in dryland regions where the irrigation ratio was below 10 percent, compared to 26 percent in regions where the irrigation ratio exceeded 50 percent. Since then, these disparities have widened. In dry regions, high-yielding varieties and heavy chemical use is much less advantageous, due to moisture problems, so farmers there have benefitted relatively little from the subsidies attached to modern inputs. Therefore, they have not been shielded from the effects of low foodgrain prices. Moreover, dryland farmers must compete with producers in more favorably endowed regions who do benefit from input subsidies (Vaidyanathan [a], 69). These unfavorable price incentives have reduced the profitability of agronomic practices, including bunding, terracing, and use of cover crops, that could raise the productivity of dryland agriculture. Although India's development strategy has included special programs for backward and dryland regions, these programs have had to contend with the differential effects of agricultural pricing policies on farms with and without irrigation.

To sum up, Indian agriculture has responded to the massive increase in demand for food. Output per capita has not only kept pace with the population; it has slightly improved to allow modest improvements in living standards. Although total caloric intake is little more than it was twenty years ago, the average Indian now has a somewhat more varied and balanced diet. Private and public investments have intensified farming practices substantially. Irrigation, partic-

ularly electrified well irrigation, has been the dri-
ving force, along with varietal improvements for
wheat and rice. Development has been highly un-
even across regions and crops, leading to somewhat wider disparities in the rural income areas.
Resource and ecological pressures have grown
perceptibly, but have not prevented continuing
increases in output and average yields. The most
intractable problems have been not technical but
institutional, having to do with coordinating the
interests and activities of different development
agencies as well as of individual cultivators, for
the common good.

Notes

1. In small areas and pilot schemes, alternative
arrangements have been tried out. In tubewell co-
operatives, water rights are assigned equally to
all member families, regardless of landholding.
Households that cannot use their share of the
water can sell it to others. (Shah, p.8.)

2. There are wide discrepancies in data from
different agencies. For example, the Planning
Commission estimates that canal irrigation increased by 9 million hectares over the same period.

V. India's Rural Off-Farm Environment

"Are not poverty and need the greatest polluters? For instance, unless we are in a position to provide employment and purchasing power for the daily necessities of the tribal people and those who live in and around our jungles, we cannot prevent them from combing the forest for food and livelihood, or from poaching and despoiling the vegetation. When they themselves feel deprived, how can we urge preservation of animals?"

Indira Gandhi, Prime Minister of India, addressing the plenary session of the UN Conference on the Human Environment, Stockholm, 1982

Although India's cropped area seems to have been expanded almost to its limits, only 140 million hectares out of the total land area of 330 million hectares are cultivated. The remaining areas of forests, woodlands, grasslands, marshes, rivers, lakes, and shorelines are known as India's Common Property Resources because rights to use and manage them are mostly held by governments or by local communities rather than by private individuals. Except for a concern about fuelwood supplies gathered mostly from natural woodlands rather than grown on plantations, the *Second India Study* paid little attention to future demands on common property resources. Nor did Indian policy-makers and planners at that time.

A. Importance of Common Property Resources

Preoccupied with raising agricultural productivity, planners probably didn't fully realize how important these non-cultivated areas were to the subsistence and livelihoods of rural households, especially to those without much land of their own. Edible fruits, nuts, berries, roots, fungi, leaves, fish, mollusks, birds and animals were gathered or hunted on these commons. Traditional medicines and natural insecticides were found in the forests. Poorer households obtained around three quarters of their fuel supplies and an even higher fraction of their animal fodder from them (Jodha [1990], Table 1, 266). This allowed households without enough crop residues from their own farms to maintain draft and milk animals. Instead of burning crop residues and animal dung, households could use them as organic manures and burn gathered fuels instead. On average, as much as 20–25 percent of the annual incomes of poor rural households came directly from Common Property (Jodha [1992], 13).

Poles and timbers for building, fibers and dyes for weaving, bark for tanning, essential oils and oil seeds, gums and resins, bamboos and canes—raw materials for artisanal crafts—could also be gathered. The common property resources offered substantial employment opportunities for the landless, for small farmers and farmworkers, especially during the off season, and for women and children. In total, smallholder households found more employment there than on their own farms. In drought years, when farming became impossible, the rural poor could fall back on the resources of forest and stream (Jodha [1992], 16). Twenty to thirty million people, many from India's tribal communities, based their livelihoods *exclusively*

49

on non-timber products obtained from forests and other common property areas (Kulkarni [1983], cited in Agarwal [1993], 11).

Of course, these uncultivated areas also served vital ecological functions that indirectly helped maintain agricultural productivity. Vegetative cover on the hillsides and plains reduced wind and water erosion and prevented the siltation of irrigation systems. The same vegetation moderated water run-off during the monsoons and preserved stream flows and wetlands during the long dry season, replenishing aquifers, irrigation tanks, and waterholes for cattle. Pollinators found refuge and nesting sites in natural areas. Farmers found rich supplies of organic manures in grasses and silts (Jodha [1992], 18–19).

The traditions and cultures of rural India are incredibly varied, but over the course of centuries, rural communities all depended on these shared natural resources. Communities that survived evolved traditions and methods for using them sustainably. In areas of settled farming, villages typically included not only the cultivated lands but the surrounding village commons, which might include forests, ponds, and pastures. The use of common resources was governed either by custom or by explicit rules: landlords or village councils sometimes set fees and appointed watchmen to regulate the use of certain valuable village resources. Villages maintained sacred groves and other natural areas, invoking religious duty to preserve certain resources. Customary practices were by and large sustainable. Typically for example, villagers would collect twigs or fallen branches for fuel and then, if necessary, lop off a few limbs, but they would not fell or destroy a living tree. Some low caste communities evolved into specialized resource users, such as fishermen, and caste membership limited access to the resource. Tribal societies in forest areas, although typically less specialized as resource users, also defined who could use the resources within its territories and how. Fallow rotations in traditional shifting cultivation were long enough to allow forests and soils to recover. Sustainability was ingrained in traditional rural societies (Agarwal [1992], 416).

B. Shrinking Common Property Resources and the Economic Effects

Much of this was altered in the 19th century and early 20th century under British rule. The colonial government asserted sovereignty over most of India's uncultivated lands, abrogating or ignoring the traditional rights and management regimes of village and tribal societies. This government designated large areas of forest as timber reserves for shipbuilding, railways and boiler fuel, and it conceded commercial timber harvesting rights in other forested areas as well (Agarwal [1992], 417). Large areas were allocated to private plantation owners and other commercial uses. In addition, population growth and irrigation investments led to large scale expansion of the cultivated area, which the colonial government encouraged as a source of additional land revenue (Tucker & Richards, Ch. 9). For all these reasons, common property resources shrank.

Independence did not reverse these trends. State and central governments retained proprietorship and authority over virtually the entire uncultivated area, inheriting the Forest Service traditions that the colonial regime had created (Gadgil, 131). Policies of the colonial era also survived, although recast as a national drive for economic development. In the forested areas, pulp and paper industries, timber production, and land for water projects and other development schemes took priority over the subsistence needs of local populations. Privatization of land for agricultural production also continued, much of it spontaneous, some of it promoted by the government through continuing irrigation and rural development investments. Spontaneous privatization usually occurred through a process of informal partitioning of parts of the commons into individual use parcels, followed gradually by appropriation of those parcels for exclusive use, and only later by legalization of private ownership of the land. In semi-arid regions spanning eight states, the area of the commons declined by 30 to 50 percent between 1950 and 1980. Taking population growth over that span into account, the area per capita declined on average by two thirds its initial extent (Jodha [1992], 21–22) *(See Figure 19.)* Since the livestock population, including more than 250 million head of cattle and buffalo, also doubled in the span of thirty-five years, pressure on available fodder and forage also intensified greatly (Bowonder, *Environmental Trends*, 3).

A broader assessment covering 16 large states (excluding the hill states of northeast India) used land use and agricultural census data to reach much the same conclusion (Chopra and Gulati, 23–24). Other than on reserve forests, cultivated lands, current fallows, and areas under non-agricultural uses, communal use rights are likely to exist by law or custom. Thus defined, the common property resource land areas of India include long-term fallow land, cultivable wastes, pastures and other grazing lands, and virtually all "protected" and unclassed forests. In most of these, institutional breakdowns and erosion of

Figure 19. Decline of Common Property Areas

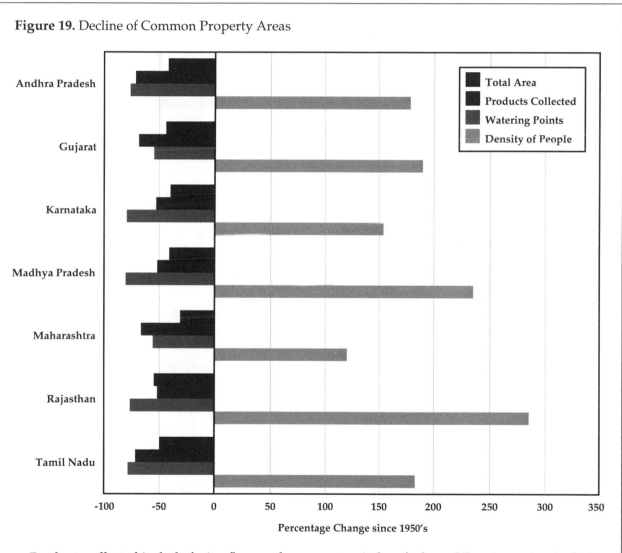

Products collected include fruits, flowers, leaves, roots, timber, fuel, etc. Watering points include grazing CPRs only.
Source: Jodha (1992).

51

governmental or village authority has increasingly opened access to the commons.

Agriculturally developed states with extensive alluvial plains, such as Punjab, Haryana, and Uttar Pradesh, have less than 10 percent of their total areas under common property regimes. At the other extreme, states that contain large areas of desert, mountain, and other uncultivable terrain, such as Rajasthan, Himachal Pradesh, and Kashmir, have the largest percentage of land in common property. In virtually all states for which data are available, the estimated extent of such land declined substantially between 1970–71 and 1986–87. Across all 16 states, the area under commons fell by 25 percent of the 1970 area; in individual states, the median decline was 9 percent.

Agriculture has expanded into uncultivated areas partially to compensate for failed attempts to redistribute holdings to the landless. Many poor or landless households couldn't hang on to lands they received because of indebtedness or shortages of credit and other needed inputs. Most common lands privatized in the first twenty years of independence fell into the hands of better-off farming households (Jodha [1992], 26). Where appropriated lands were able to support continuing cropping or where management of fodder and forage improved, privatization raised productivity and output. However, in many sub-marginal lands, erosion and nutrient depletion on lands converted to agriculture continued the process of soil degradation that deforestation had begun (Jodha [1992], 28).

Although government continued to assert authority over the remaining commons at the expense of local communities, their ability to enforce restrictions on access and use eroded under the pressure of local demands. As the resource base shrank and population expanded, forest officials found themselves increasingly cast as guards and police, fighting a rearguard action against "encroachment" by local people seeking access to resources they badly needed and had traditionally used. In the villages, resentment against the government's much more favorable treatment of large-scale industrial interests in access to common property resources often ran high (Agarwal [1992], 423; Gadgil [1990], 139). With weakened authority over the commons, village councils—now locally elected but often driven by factional conflicts—were also less able to limit exploitation. For such reasons, common property resources that had once been managed more or less sustainably through local traditions and community authorities increasingly became open to unregulated exploitation by all. Inevitably, "open access" to these resources tended toward a situation akin to Garrett Hardin's famous "tragedy of the commons," wherein no individual had reason to restrain his own use, knowing that others were free to exploit the common resources without limit (Agarwal [1993], 4).

When remaining areas of common property resources couldn't meet the demands on them sustainably, a cycle of continuing degradation was set in motion. As more people and animals sought sustenance on a smaller resource base, exploitation only intensified.

These forces did not operate uniformly across rural India. The commons were better preserved in more remote villages where traditions of self-reliance had been maintained, where socio-economic differentials had not widened, and where government programs and commercial forces had penetrated less thoroughly. They persisted to a greater extent in less-favored agricultural regions, where common property resources were essential to subsistence (Chopra & Gulati, 13). Still, when remaining areas of common property resources couldn't meet the demands on them sustainably, a cycle of continuing degradation was set in motion. Overexploitation reduced the stock of trees and useful plants and of fish and animals. As more people and animals sought sustenance on a smaller resource base, exploitation only intensified. As productivity declined, community management received less support, especially from better-off households with other options than to use common resources (Jodha [1992], 45–47).

Although the area officially under forests (that is, under the authority of Forest Agencies) has been maintained, forest cover and tree stocks have greatly diminished (Gadgil, 137). Most of the vast natural teak and "sal" forests have given way to open scrub. Perennial grasses useful as fodder have been replaced with unpalatable bushes and barren patches. Many waterholes and tanks have silted or dried up. In coastal areas, coral reefs teeming with life have been destroyed by siltation, pollution, or limestone mining. Mangroves have been cleared for fuelwood, salt flats, or shrimp farms, destroying marine breeding grounds. This downward spiral has created vast areas of wastelands (Chopra & Gulati, 2). Although comprehensive data on resource degradation is absent, the evidence from widespread village surveys is persuasive.

C. Effects on Rural Poverty

Villagers have adapted to the decline of the commons as their means and opportunities allowed (Jodha [1992], 45–54). Better-off households have substituted other resources, especially where irrigation has allowed more intensive farming. Buffalos, stall-fed on residues from the higher crop yields, have been replacing cattle grazed on the commons as milk animals. Tractors have been replacing bullocks as draft animals. Chemical fertilizers have been substituted for organic manures. Where commercial farming is prevalent, wage labor and monetary transactions have replaced reciprocal obligations to maintain and use the commons. Landowners have withdrawn traditional privileges for communal grazing on their lands after harvest or during short fallow periods, for example. As better-off households have withdrawn from the commons, they have also become less interested in their maintenance, except where opportunities for privatization have arisen or government incentives have been available.

For poorer households, the options have been much more limited. These households spend much more time collecting fuel and fodder, at the expense of other productive activities. In regions where fuelwood is scarce, they burn dung and plant residues that would have been used as organic manures. When necessary, they have adopted strategies of desperation, severely lopping or felling trees, digging up roots of shrubs that might otherwise have regenerated, or using plants that were previously shunned. Many replace cattle and buffalos with sheep and goats, which can forage more successfully on degraded lands and sparse vegetation, although these small ruminants are much harder on the ecosystem in the long run.

Since most of the goods and services obtained from the commons are gathered by household labor, rather than purchased on local markets, surveys of household consumption expenditures haven't fully reflected their increasing scarcity. Since these goods and services have become scarcer, surveys measuring household living standards in terms of household spending may overstate improvements. Some households have been forced to purchase substitutes for goods once available freely or to do without some of the goods that they used to be able to collect in the commons (Agarwal [1993], 37–47). The impoverishment of the rural environment has offset some of the gains realized from increased agricultural output and rural wage employment.

The loss of common property resources has hit women and girls especially hard. They traditionally have had much of the responsibility for gathering fuelwood, fodder and water. As boys have increasingly been kept in school, girls have also taken on more of the burden of tending animals (Agarwal [1993], 41). Since women typically have greater access to common property resources in rural areas than to privately owned land or other assets, the degradation and shrinkage of the commons has undermined women's economic base disproportionately. As the commons shrink, women and girls must spend ever more time gathering needed fuel, fodder, and water, losing hours that could have been spent in other pro-

Since women typically have greater access to common property resources in rural areas than to privately owned land or other assets, the degradation and shrinkage of the commons has undermined women's economic base disproportionately.

ductive activities. Materials that could have been gathered for sale or for crafts have become scarce. And, as the number of animals that can be sustained on the commons has fallen, an important source of income and nutrition has been eroded.

Women's vulnerability to the loss of common property resources varies by region (Agarwal [1993], 19). The situation is more serious where gender bias is severe—in the northern, northwestern, and eastern states—because there women have less access to agricultural land, job opportunities, and other resources. In states where gender discrimination is compounded by widespread poverty, women's vulnerability is greater still. Where common property resources are also inherently scarce because the climate is harsh or the ecosystem barren, the situation is worst of all.

Fortunately, these worst-case conditions do not occur simultaneously all over India. In the Punjab, for example, gender bias is quite strong and the semi-arid climate and the dominance of private agricultural holdings make common resources scarce, but economic development has made poverty relatively rare. In Orissa, poverty is more widespread and gender bias is also pronounced, but abundant rainfall makes biomass and water resources less scarce. The greatest vulnerability is found in such states as Rajasthan, Bihar, and in much of Uttar Pradesh, where conditions are relatively unfavorable on all three counts. Over time, these regional differences have changed little, except that development has re-

duced poverty and (to some extent) gender bias in the agriculturally advanced states of the Punjab and Haryana, in Gujarat, and in West Bengal (Agarwal [1993], 33–35).

D. Effects on Biodiversity

In addition to its adverse effects on the rural poor, and especially on poor women, the degradation of common property resources has severely damaged India's unusually diverse populations of living things. About 80,000 species of animals and 15,000 species of flowering plants have already been identified in India, but tens of thousands more species remain virtually unknown (Gadgil & Homji, 175). Because of its size, the variety of its climates and landforms, and its relative isolation beneath the Himalayas, India is one of the "megadiversity" countries, home to unusually large numbers of endemic species. However, because most of India's distinct ecological zones have been destroyed or extensively disturbed, and now exist only in scattered remnant patches, many of India's unique plants and animals are threatened or endangered.

Even in 1972, when the *Second India Study* was underway, the government listed 70 mammals, 22 reptiles and amphibians, and 41 birds as rare and highly endangered under the Wildlife Protection Act (Kirloskar Consultants, 229). The mammalian list included virtually all of India's large predator species, which require substantial ranges in which to hunt: the Indian lion, tiger, spotted leopard, clouded leopard, snow leopard, lynx, Malabar civet, Indian wolf, cheetah, and the golden, fishing, desert, leopard, marbled, and rusty-spotted cats. Also rare or endangered were many forest-dwelling primates, such as the slow loris, the capped langur, the crab-eating maqaque, the leaf monkey, the hoolock gibbon, and the lion-tailed maqaque. Other victims of deforestation were the small Travancore flying squirrel, lesser panda, sun bear, sloth bear, pygmy hog, Andaman wild pig, and spotted linsang. Habitat loss had also endangered many grazing and herding animals, including the Indian elephant and rhinoceros, the black buck, the

Indian and Tibetan gazelles, Himalayan ibex, Himalayan and Nilgiri tahrs, Indian wild ass, Kashmir stag, wild buffalo, wild yak, and the brow-antlered, mouse, and musk deers. Despite concerted efforts to save such flagship species as the lion, tiger, and wild elephant, continuing deforestation at the rate of 150,000 to 300,000 hectares per year over the past 20 years and other encroachments into natural habitat have heightened threats to India's diverse mammals.

Degradation of India's coastal ecosystems, rivers and wetlands had put many other species on the endangered list as far back as 1972. These included several unique to India, such as the Ganges dolphin, the Ganges soft-shelled turtle, the crocodile-like gharial, the white-bellied sea eagle, the Andaman teal, and the pinkheaded duck. India's bird life is extraordinarily rich, in part because many Asian species from north of the Himalayas, such as the endangered Siberian white crane, winter in India's plains and marshes. The continued loss of habitat has threatened many, such as the Great Indian bustard and the forest-dwelling pied Indian hornbill. The continuing large-scale use of such bioaccumulating pesticides as DDT has endangered many falcons, hawks, osprey, lammergeier, and other raptor species. Although information on the numbers of these endangered species is scarce, the underlying threats to their survival have intensified over the past 20 years.

The remaining unconnected patches of relatively intact natural ecosystems—mostly in protected areas—average only 1,100 square kilometers in extent. With few exceptions, sanctuaries and protected areas amount to only a few percent of the original ecological zones. Most are surrounded by settled or disturbed areas, so they are thus highly vulnerable to incursions or invasion from the surrounding regions by growing populations or commercial interests. In most of India's protected areas, tensions between resource managers and land-scarce impoverished neighbors or opportunistic commercial developers are chronic. These remnant patches—surrounded as they are—are also vulnerable to possible future changes in climate since the plant and animal

With few exceptions, sanctuaries and protected areas amount to only a few percent of the original ecological zones. These remnant patches—surrounded as they are—are also vulnerable to possible future changes in climate since the plant and animal communities that make up the ecosystems will have nowhere to migrate if the climate zone to which they are adapted shifts.

communities that make up the ecosystems will have nowhere to migrate if the climate zone to which they are adapted shifts.

Since the *Second India Study* was completed, government policies toward common property resources have shifted significantly. Several large-scale development efforts have been organized to promote reforestation and watershed management (Jodha [1992], 69). Environmental protection laws and programs have been created to control water pollution (Bowonder, *Environmental Regulations*, 2). Forest policies have been revised to emphasize community over commercial interests. In 11 states, community user-groups have been given exclusive access rights to non-timber forest products in exchange for their participation in forest protection activities. A number of local initiatives and pilot programs have clearly demonstrated that affirming local community's rights, assuring them access to common property resources, and increasing local community participation in management decisions, promotes sustainable resource use. Many community initiatives have been started, organized, and sustained by local women, who have most at stake. Affirming equitable rules of participation and access seems to be a critical element in improving local management and halting environmental degradation.

VI. Urbanization, Urban Poverty, and the Urban Environment

The *Second India Study* authors were gravely concerned about the urban bias in India's development patterns, which had created enormous disparities in living standards between citydwellers and villagers and which they saw as the source of an irresistible pull toward the cities. To some extent their concern has been validated by subsequent events. Over the past 20 years cities have grown at least as fast as the *Second India Study* anticipated, and the disparity between per capita production in rural and urban areas has widened. *(See Figure 20.)* The urban economy now produces one-half of India's GDP. But, urban poverty has emerged as a major problem that the *Second India Study* didn't fully anticipate. The number of desperately poor people living in cities has increased much faster than the number of rural poor. For these people, the quality of the urban environment can be a matter of life or death. There is a widening gap between the need for essential urban services and their availability. The spread of urban poverty and the deterioration of the urban environment are becoming more salient issues in India's development (GOI, Planning Commission [1992]).

A. Urbanization Patterns

India's urban population was 217 million in 1991—26 percent of the total and somewhat more than the *Second India Study*'s forecast of 210 million. Since 1971, the urban population has doubled, increasing at twice the rate of the rural population (Mathur, 6). Although India's urban-

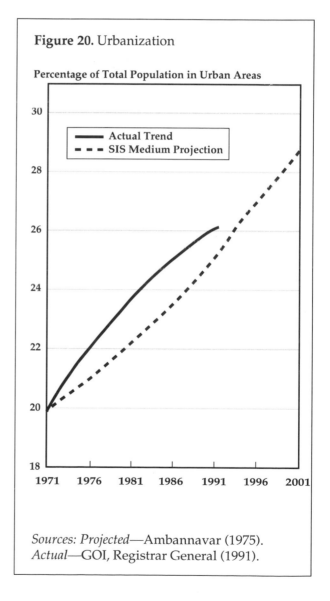

Figure 20. Urbanization

Percentage of Total Population in Urban Areas

Sources: Projected—Ambannavar (1975).
Actual—GOI, Registrar General (1991).

ization has not been particularly rapid by developing-country standards, 100 million people—the equivalent of eight Calcuttas—have been added to the urban scene.

However, the image of landless peasants pouring into the cities from an overpopulated countryside is distorted. The 1981 census found only 29 percent of the population living outside their place of birth, and less than 20 percent of these migrants had moved from a rural area to a city. A rising fraction of urban population growth is the result of natural increase, the excess of births over deaths among citydwellers: two-thirds of the cities' growth in the 1980s, compared to two-fifths in the 1970s (Mathur, 11, Table 5). Although birth and death rates are both lower in urban areas than in the countryside, urban population growth from natural increase still averaged about 2 percent over the period, only slightly lower than the overall population growth rate. Most of the states in which urban growth has been especially rapid are those in which birth rates remain high.

India's urban scene is no longer one of towns and overgrown villages. Now, two thirds of the urban population live in genuine cities with populations over 100,000. One third live in cities of a million inhabitants or more, up from one quarter in 1971. There were 9 such cities in India in 1971, 23 in 1991, and no less than 50 are expected by the end of the century (Mathur, 7–8). Even the largest cities are still growing. In the West, such metropolises as London and New York are stable in size or are even losing population, but the combined population of Calcutta, Bombay, and Delhi—India's largest cities—has doubled since 1971.

Growth on this scale has put enormous pressure on urban infrastructure and administration. Housing, water supplies, sewage and water treatment systems, roads and public transportation, schools, hospitals and health centers, to say nothing of factories, offices and shops, were needed on a vast scale to accommodate a city population increasing faster than 3.5 percent per year. The task was rendered more desperate by the fact that

in 1971, conditions in most cities were even worse. H. Ezekiel, one of the *Second India Study* authors, noted that in Calcutta, an estimated two-thirds of the population lived in shacks, hovels, and substandard structures, while in Bombay, at least 350,000 people—6 percent of the population at the time—lived on the pavement (Mathur, 3).

Unlike several Asian countries where most of the urban growth has taken place in the capital city, India's is dispersed throughout the country (Mathur, 7, Table 9). In particular, urbanization has not occurred only in the richest or most developed states. On the contrary, during the past 20 years it has been most rapid in those regions where only a relatively small fraction of the population lived in cities in 1971, where the birth rate was high, and where poverty was relatively widespread. Contrary to the fears expressed in the *Second India Study*, the "pull" of rapid economic growth and of development policies biased in favor of urban areas have not been prominent influences on the pace of urbanization. Instead, many of the states in which urban growth was rapid, such as Orissa, Uttar Pradesh, and Rajasthan, lagged behind the national average in economic growth; many of the states in which economic growth was the fastest—Maharashtra, Karnataka, and Tamil Nadu—recorded relatively slow rates of urban growth (Mathur, 15, Graph 2). Therefore, the poorer states have been catching up in their degree of urbanization.

B. Urban Poverty

Urban poverty persists partly because of rapid urban growth in poverty-stricken states and the dominant role of natural increase in city growth. Within the cities, poorer and less educated households tended to be those with the highest birth rates. Slow economic development, and, in particular, slow growth of industrial output and employment, failed to provide the engine that could pull these rapidly increasing urban populations out of poverty. Overwhelmingly, low income households in cities depend on their own labor for survival; industrial growth provides not only the direct factory employment, but also the ancillary opportunities in transportation, trade, construction, and other services that provide jobs for the urban poor. Because industry grew slowly and also became increasingly capital-intensive over most of this 20-year period, the way out of poverty is closed to most of these people. Only during the 1980s did industrial output accelerate, and even then it spurred little direct employment.

The working definition of poverty in India is very basic; it is whether a household's income is sufficient for it to purchase enough calories for adequate nutrition, given typical prices, expenditures and dietary patterns in the locality. Careful estimates of the number of households below the poverty line take account of price differentials, differing caloric needs in rural and urban areas, and different expenditure patterns across regions. However, this measure does not encompass other aspects of economic wellbeing and security; whether a household has assets or sources of support it can draw on; whether it is in debt; whether or not the household can obtain essential items, such as fuel and water, outside the cash economy; or whether the household's immediate surroundings create risks to health and productivity (Chambers [1992], 310–313).

Even defining poverty simply in terms of a household's ability to purchase enough calories, 40 percent of the urban population fell below the poverty line in 1987–88. Although the situation was worse in 1973–74, when one-half the urban population lived in poverty, the *numbers* of urban poor still grew from 60 to 84 million. By contrast, in rural areas the *numbers* of poor fell from 261 to 229 million, and the incidence of poverty fell from 56 to 39 percent of the rural population (Mathur, 18). A much larger fraction of India's poor now live in urban areas than in the early 1970s. By the late 1980s, for the first time, the fraction of the population below the poverty line became higher in cities than in rural areas, even though output per capita is far higher in cities.

The interplay of underlying economic and demographic conditions largely determined the extent of poverty in each region. In Bihar, one of the poorest states, poverty afflicted over half the urban dwellers; in the Punjab, a relatively rich state, only 12 percent lived in poverty. The urban poor tended to increase in numbers more rapidly over the period in states experiencing rapid urbanization and relatively slow economic growth, as one might expect (Mathur, 26).

C. Environmental Hazards and Effects on Health

These trends exacerbated pressures on the urban environment, and, hence, worsened living conditions for the urban poor. Population densities in cities increased by 20 percent between 1971 and 1991, forcing up urban land values and making it increasingly difficult for low income households to find space. In the 23 largest cities, 28 percent of the people now live in squatter settlements, twice the percentage for all of India (Bowonder, *Population*, 28). Housing in these settlements is typically makeshift, constructed from scrap material—sometimes just rags and straw. Only one household in twenty in these "bustee" settlements enjoys a "pucca" house of permanent construction. Most of the squatter settlements are established on undesirable land—subject to flooding, near heavily polluted industrial sites or other hazards. The catastrophic toll of death and injury to slumdwellers in an industrial area of Bhopal when a pesticide-manufacturing plant accidentally released toxic chemicals demonstrated how precarious such industrial residential areas can be. Moreover, very few have sewers, drains, or facilities for collecting and disposing of garbage and other solid wastes—ideal conditions for the spread of communicable diseases. On the other hand, in some of the largest cities, such as Calcutta, the quality of life is better now than when the *Second India Study* was written.

In particular, progress has also been made in providing access to safe water in Indian cities. According to official statistics, almost 90 percent of the urban population now has access to protected drinking water, compared to 78 percent in 1981, although for the urban poor the source is typically a public tap and supplies may not be sufficient (Mathur, Table 21). Yet, rivers and streams bordering urban settlements, still widely used for bathing and washing, are heavily polluted by human and industrial wastes, as are shallow aquifers underlying cities, from which many households draw well water. In coastal cities that have overdrawn their groundwater supplies, such as Madras, the intrusion of saltwater into the aquifers has created serious water supply problems. Heavy pollution loadings and increasing urban population growth have compounded the problems of providing adequate water supplies.

Less progress has been made in the collection and treatment of human wastes, which can be inordinately expensive if conventional sewer systems and sewage treatment plants are used. Over half the urban population, 125 million people, have no access to basic sanitary facilities, but must make use of "open spaces" surrounding slum settlements (NIUA, cited in Mathur, Table 25). This fosters the spread of fecal-borne diseases, such as dysentery, hepatitis, helminthic infections, and cholera. According to 1988 data, in cities with populations of 100,000 or more, only 22 percent of the sewage generated was collected, and, of that, only 62 percent received primary and secondary treatment. Of the 241 towns with fewer than 100,000 inhabitants, which contain one third the urban population, only 19 have wastewater collection systems, and only 10 have treatment facilities (GOI Central Pollution Control Board, cited in Bowonder, *Water*, Tables 6–8).

The urban poor are exposed to other environmental hazards. Most still rely on fuelwood and biomass fuels, which they must purchase at rising prices in the marketplace. Around most Indian cities, forest cover has been disappearing at the rate of 2–3 percent per year (Bowonder [1985], cited in Mathur, Table 18). A wide ring of deforestation has spread, as all nearby fuelwood sources have been exhausted. Women cooking with these fuels in tiny huts, using makeshift inefficient stoves, are exposed to incredible concentrations of smoke, as are their children: 25,000 micrograms per cubic meter according to a study carried out in Ahmedabad. The consequences include high levels of bronchitis and respiratory infections, which are often fatal in malnourished young children, and widespread chronic eye irritation and infection.

In the 20 years since the Second India Study, *the number of vehicles on the road in India has increased tenfold.*

Because so many squatter settlements are clustered in industrial areas, along roadways, and in other congested urban areas, the urban poor are highly exposed to air pollution from vehicles and industries. In the 20 years since the *Second India Study*, the number of vehicles on the road in India has increased tenfold, and city traffic jams are commonplace. Two thirds of the vehicles on the road, almost all in urban areas, are two-wheel motor rickshaws and scooters powered by high emissions two-stroke engines. Poorly maintained buses and trucks spew forth highly toxic diesel emissions. Gasoline in India still contains lead, and lead concentrations found in samples taken from India's children are extremely high. A study carried out in Ahmedabad, Bangalore, and Calcutta found that lead concentrations in the blood averaged twice as high as in other large cities where unleaded gas was used, such as Tokyo and Stockholm (Khandekar, 46–49). Exposure to lead impairs children's mental development. In Bombay, where trend data are available, total atmospheric emissions of sulphur dioxide, nitrogen oxides, suspended particulates, and carbon monoxide doubled between 1970–71 and 1985–86 (Punder & Das [1985]). Measured air pollution from particulates and NO_x, which are vehicle related, have risen in almost all major Indian cities. *(See Figures 21, 22 and 23.)*

These environmental hazards are particularly dangerous to the urban poor because they compound the problems of malnutrition, general ill-health, and the lack of medical care. The well known interplay of diarrhea, weight loss, and

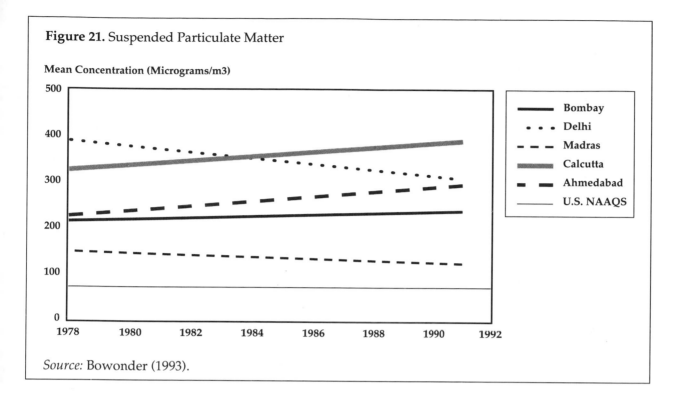

Figure 21. Suspended Particulate Matter

Mean Concentration (Micrograms/m3)

Bombay
Delhi
Madras
Calcutta
Ahmedabad
U.S. NAAQS

Source: Bowonder (1993).

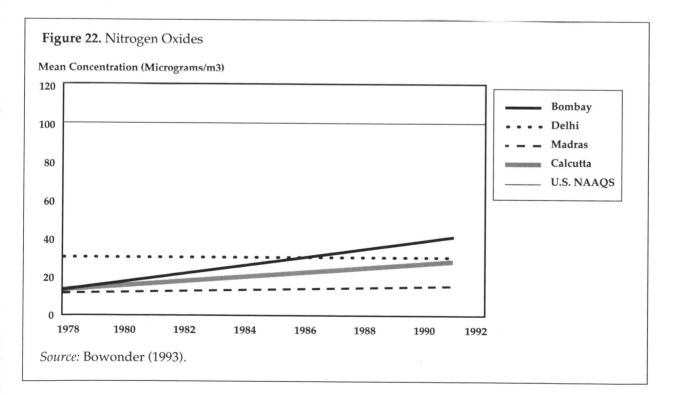

Figure 22. Nitrogen Oxides

Mean Concentration (Micrograms/m3)

Bombay
Delhi
Madras
Calcutta
U.S. NAAQS

Source: Bowonder (1993).

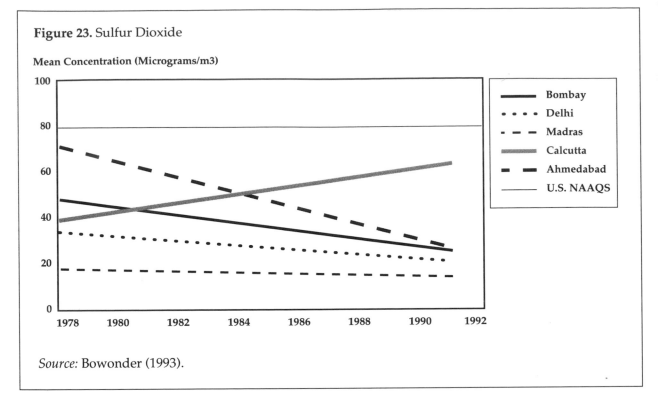

Figure 23. Sulfur Dioxide

Mean Concentration (Micrograms/m3)

Legend:
- Bombay
- Delhi
- Madras
- Calcutta
- Ahmedabad
- U.S. NAAQS

Source: Bowonder (1993).

malnutrition, and vulnerability to respiratory infection is a deadly cycle to which many Indian children succumb. The prevalence of tuberculosis which spreads mainly among low income populations living in close contact, is 30 percent higher in India than in developing countries as a whole. To this must be added the risks of exposure to high concentrations of air pollutants, known to have more serious harmful effects on those whose respiratory functions are already impaired. A WHO/UNEP study compared standardized prevalences of respiratory diseases in different areas of Bombay, classified according to ambient average concentrations of sulphur dioxide. The study found that relative prevalence of most respiratory diseases were higher in polluted urban areas than in the rural control area which had no sanitation, no protected water supply, and poorer housing and medical care than Bombay. (*See Table 2*, from Bowonder, *Air Pollution*, Table 21.) As a result, infant mortality rates in urban slums in 1989 were 123 per thousand, compared to the all-India rate of 98, the overall urban rate of 62, and an infant mortality rate of 22 among urban households above the poverty line (Srinivasan, Table 7; Mathur, Table 26).

In addition, these conditions impose a heavy burden of ill health on the living. The results of a study of women's health in a Bombay slum suggest the extent of the problem at the time of the survey:

"...that 70 to 75 percent of the women suffer from anaemia, 50 to 60 percent suffer from chronic malnutrition and B-complex vitamin deficiency, 25 to 30 percent suffer from repeated attacks of gastroenteritis and infestations of worms, 15 percent complain of upper respiratory tract infections, and 13 to 15 percent suffer from skin infections like scabies, pediculosis, and pyoderma. Apart from these common ailments, they also suffer from pulmonary tuberculosis, urinary tract infection, typhoid fever, infectious hepatitis, malaria and such chronic diseases as diabetes and hypertension." (*The Economic Times*, 28–4–85).

Table 2. Ratios of Disease Prevalence in Bombay to Rural Control Sample

	Pollutant Load in Urban Areas			
Disease	Area #1 Less than 50 microgrammes per cubic meter	Area #2 51–100 microgrammes per cubic meter	Area #3 More than 100 microgrammes per cubic meter	Rural Control Sample
Dyspnea	0.58	1.09	1.33	1.00
Chronic Cough	0.52	0.82	1.55	1.00
Intermittent Cough	0.11	1.57	4.22	1.00
Frequent Colds	1.10	1.89	1.64	1.00
Chronic Bronchitis	0.46	0.90	0.90	1.00
Cardiac Disorders	3.04	1.59	2.52	1.00

Source: WHO/UNEP (1992).

This overwhelming burden of sickness cannot but lower the productivity and earnings of adults who must work every day for a living, and perpetuates poverty in these unhealthy environments. Women in particular, who suffer from inferior access to health care and even to food, but who nonetheless must work long hours, are soon debilitated. Children, who also suffer chronic sickness, malnutrition, and vitamin deficiency, cannot attend school and learn effectively if they are sick and hungry, so their hopes of escaping poverty's trap are also undermined.

State and national development programs over this period focussed increasingly on poverty alleviation. During the 1980s, combatting urban poverty became an explicit focus of development programs. New programs were put in place in the Seventh Five-Year Plan to improve environmental conditions in urban slums, provide basic health services, especially for women and children; and support microenterprises and generate employment for the urban poor. Although most such programs were planned and implemented in a top-down fashion, more than ten million people had benefitted from these interventions by 1991. Targeted anti-poverty programs supplemented ongoing efforts to expand the availability of urban services and infrastructure, but were insufficient in scale or impact to stem the increase

in the numbers of urban poor (Mathur, 50).

Moreover, these efforts were held back by important urban policy and institutional issues, as well as the overall demographic and economic trends. Over the period, municipal governments became ever weaker, their authority and functions progressively taken over by state governments and state sponsored urban development agencies. As the role of local governments in planning and providing urban services diminished, accountability and popular participation suffered (Mohan, 1917–1919). Municipalities became financially more dependent on transfers and grants from state and federal governments, which controlled the important tax bases, since few taxes devolved to local government. Property taxes, the municipalities' own principal revenue source, stagnated not only because of inefficient assessment and collection procedures but also because urban rent control froze property taxes at artificially low levels. Urban services deteriorated as responsibilities for maintaining infrastructure planned and constructed by state agencies outstripped municipalities' financial resources.

During the 1970s and 1980s, user charges played almost no role in financing urban infrastructure or in rationing the growing use of scarce urban services. In the absence of direct service charges, cost recovery was usually through surcharges on property taxes, a practice that multiplied all the limitations of property taxes. User charges rarely even covered operating and maintenance costs, and made no contribution to capital needs. Most capital spending consisted of public sector budgetary outlays financed by transfers from state and central government, and ultimately paid for by general taxes. Urban services have been heavily subsidized, even for members of the urban middle class who can afford to pay. Consequently, the availability and quality of service for most of the urban poor is low. For example, public transportation and urban road networks have deteriorated while private vehicles have multiplied, aggravating congestion and pollution (GOI, Planning Commission, Ch. 13). Revenues were estimated in the 1980s to cover only half of minimal current expenditures, including depreciation (NIUA [1983]). Capital infrastructure met only one quarter to one third of estimated minimal needs.

Municipalities have had little financial autonomy to set user charges, even had they been motivated to do so. Any revenues from user charges have been merged with other receipts in municipal accounts, not reserved for improving or expanding services. Thus, agencies supplying urban services have been able to generate few financial resources internally, either for capital or maintenance expenditures, and have not been financially accountable to their customers. Without any dedicated revenue source, they have not been able to tap financial markets as autonomous borrowers, nor have they been able to involve the private sector. Little institutional or financial strength has been created with which to meet the infrastructure demands of rapidly growing cities (Mohan, 1919).

Other aspects of the legal and regulatory framework for urban development unintentionally impeded the supply of urban land and housing. Rent control not only froze property tax revenues but also discouraged investment in urban housing. Laws imposing ceilings on urban landholdings, land acquisition, and transfers also impeded commercial real estate investment and the development of building sites. For example, owners of land in excess of the ceiling are not permitted to build on it, although they have through a variety of means forestalled state governments from taking it over. Paradoxically, the long-run effects of regulations put in place to prevent profiteering in urban real estate has been to drive land and property values up out of reach of lower income households.

Partly by policy decision and partly by default, more urban services are being taken over by private companies and contractors. In Calcutta, for example, after an experiment in nationalizing urban public transportation failed, the sector was opened to all sorts of private buses, minibuses, taxis and other vehicles. Two-thirds of daily trips are now by bus, and private companies provide 90 percent of them (Roy [1988]). In Madras, more than 170 neighborhood civic associations contract with private rubbish collecting firms, who sweep streets, collect rubbish, remove recyclables, and deliver the rest to the municipal landfill. To date, however, such examples represent more an adaptation to the municipalities' failure to provide adequate services than a solution to the serious problems that exist. Stronger municipal agencies, revenue and tax reform, and market mechanisms are all needed to provide an increasing urban population with adequate services.

In summary, the growth of India's cities since 1971 proceeded in a predictable pattern and at a normal pace. What was unforeseen was the rapid increase in the numbers of urban poor, which stemmed from continued population growth, the slow overall growth of the economy, the stagnation of industrial employment, and the wide disparities in urban incomes. Poverty would itself consign tens of millions of households to squalid living conditions, but their plight was more precarious because public authorities couldn't keep up with the growing demand for essential urban services or prevent urban pollution from increasing. These lags in infrastructure investment stemmed from a progressive weakening of municipal authorities and from urban development policies that chronically failed to produce needed revenues.

VII. Energy, Population, and the Environment

Even in the early 1970s, the *Second India Study* recognized clearly some of the most important energy problems that India would confront over the next 20 years. The first of these was the critical shortage of traditional biomass fuels in rural India, which was both the cause and the result of serious ecological degradation even then. The second was India's unbalanced fossil energy resources of abundant low-quality coal but relatively meager petroleum reserves. With demands for liquid fuels rising rapidly, the fear was that this imbalance would leave India economically vulnerable to rising oil prices. The third, from the perspective of the *Second India Study*, was the very low per capita consumption of energy, which was associated with low per capita incomes and low productivity in agriculture, transportation, and other sectors of the economy. This posed the substantial problem of raising the supply of useful energy.

A. The *Second India Study*'s Assessment

The *Second India Study* identified potential technological solutions to these problems. Grounded in the dominant central planning philosophy of the period, the study indicated what shifts in priorities and allocations were needed. However, developments in the energy sector have diverged substantially from the technological pathways the study identified. In part, the differences can be attributed to unforeseen structural changes in the Indian economy and

developments in the energy sector. Mainly, however, the divergences are grounded in institutional and policy issues that the *Second India Study* didn't fully address but which have strongly influenced how poverty and population growth affected resource use.

In 1971, over half of India's total energy supplies came from overused biomass fuel resources. The "high population—low growth" scenario discussed in the *Second India Study* energy report (economic growth averaging 5.5 percent annually through the end of the century, and the population approaching 1.1 billion by 2001), which is close to the actual trajectories of demographic and economic change, has meant more people in rural areas, where biomass fuels dominate, and a slower penetration of the commercial fuels used by better-off households. For both these reasons, the *Second India Study* anticipated that—absent vigorous countermeasures—more firewood, animal dung, and crop residues would be burned year after year, exacerbating an already serious biofuel deficit (Parikh [1976], 91). Even in the early 1970s, the authorized fuelwood harvesting from forests controlled by the forest departments met less than 10 percent of estimated firewood consumption. The rest came from incursions into these forests and from the harvest of wood on other uncultivated lands in excess of annual growth and reafforestation. The consequent thinning of the forest stock, the *Second India Study* warned, would be "very damaging to both soil fertility and ecological balance." Substantial fractions of animal dung and animal residues were also being burnt as fuel to meet the rural energy deficit despite their value as organic manures. The dangers to the soil's structure, water-holding capacity, and nutrient content from a loss of organic material were foreseen. Excessive burning of biomass was an obvious link among population growth, poverty, and the environment.

India's growing dependence on petroleum imports was an equally clear link between energy and economic development. At the time of the *Second India Study*, petroleum consumption was growing at 9 percent per year, more than twice the rate of coal (Parikh [1976], 17). Yet, two thirds of India's oil was imported, and proven reserves at that time amounted to less than ten times India's still low annual consumption. Even before the second round of oil price increases in the late 1970s and early 1980s, the *Second India Study* saw the need to substitute coal for petroleum wherever feasible, restrain the growth of demand for petroleum products, and explore potential domestic oil and gas resources. Otherwise, it was realized, oil imports would put impossible pressures on the balance of payments, limiting supplies of other critical industrial materials and imported capital goods. One *Second India Study* scenario incorporated all reasonable technological possibilities to cut back on petroleum use. It implied that historical growth rates could be reversed: the growth of oil consumption could fall to 5 percent per year, and coal and electricity use could rise annually by 9 and 10 percent, respectively. Even so, the study calculated, one third of India's foreign exchange earnings over the period would have to be devoted to petroleum imports, even if exports grew by 7 percent per year (Parikh [1976], 128).

The third major challenge the *Second India Study* foresaw was creating the capacity to meet the rapidly rising demands for commercial energy implied by projected economic and population growth. India in 1971, the study pointed out, consumed energy equivalent to only 189 kgs. of coal per person per year, less than one fiftieth the level of consumption in the United States—and half of India's energy use was based on non-commercial fuels. At the same time, annual per

capita income in India, expressed in U.S. dollars, was hardly more than the average American's weekly income. The *Second India Study* argued that rapid economic growth would require even more rapid increases in commercial energy use. Agricultural expansion would depend almost entirely on yield increases, which would come from increased use of agricultural chemicals, from irrigation pumping, and from farm mechanization. Industrialization along the lines of Planning Commission models would require substantial expansions of metals, machinery, and chemicals industries, which were themselves energy-intensive and also required large-scale transportation and infrastructure development. Population growth, rising *per capita* incomes, and urbanization would create rapidly growing demands for rural and urban electricity networks, for kerosene for lighting, and for other commercial fuels. Thus, according to the *Second India Study*, coal use would increase ten fold between 1970–71 and the end of the century, petroleum use five times, and electricity use 12.5 times (Parikh [1976], 127). Although it was recognized that meeting these energy demands would strain both investment and foreign exchange budgets, much more attention was paid to the mix of fuels and energy technologies that supply energy in these amounts than to the possibilities for energy conservation or demand management.

The *Second India Study* pointed the way toward *technological* solutions to these energy problems (Parikh [1976], 115). In rural areas, the solution lay in replacing inefficient and overexploited traditional fuels and conversion devices with more efficient alternatives. Biogas plants, which convert animal dung and other organic wastes to methane and nitrogenous fertilizer through anaerobic fermentation, were seen as an important and highly attractive option. They could raise the energy recovery from organic wastes tremendously, both for clean burning fuel and fertilizer, and could be built at small scales with relatively low capital costs and simple technology. Twelve million rural households, those with enough animals to supply individual plants, would find biogas plants an attractive investment for lighting and cooking; many of the remaining

78 percent of rural households could be served by biogas plants constructed and operated by village communities (Parikh [1976], 101). Biogas plants could also fuel as many as 21 million additional pumpsets drawing irrigation water from underground aquifers. In addition, it was anticipated that by the end of the century, 80 percent of rural households would have electricity, mainly for lighting, but electricity could also energize as many as 15 million pumps.

The other major option cited for meeting rural energy needs was fuelwood plantations. With typical yields, the *Second India Study* estimated, 50 acres under plantations could fully meet a village's energy needs (Parikh [1976], 91–92). This substantial land requirement could be reduced by an order of magnitude if high-yielding tree species suitable for dryland plantations could be found and used. For urban households still burning fuelwood brought in from the countryside, soft coal briquettes could provide a cheap alternative fuel. In combination, plantations, electrification, and biogas plants could meet rural energy needs even under the "High population-Low growth" scenario while reducing pressure on biomass resources.

The most urgent challenges and best opportunities for reducing the growth of oil demand lay in the transportation sector. The increasing share of freight moving by truck could be reversed by investing in railways and improving their efficiency. Railways could be converted from diesel to electricity. Rapidly growing automotive traffic could be curtailed, and urban transportation could be made more efficient by investing heavily in buses, light rail, and other forms of public transportation. If urban growth were also channeled into medium-sized, high-density cities, transportation needs could be further scaled down (Parikh [1976], 114).

In industry, using coal instead of fuel oil for process heat, electricity for motive power, coal gas as a feedstock for fertilizer plants, and railways for transportation were the important technical options for cutting petroleum use (Parikh [1976], 128). The direct industrial use of coal was projected to rise rapidly to 200 million tons by 1990–91, and—under India's strategy of import-substituting, heavy industrialization—45 percent of that was expected to supply the steel industry's open hearth furnaces and coke-ovens.

Electricity output overall was projected to rise rapidly from 49 billion kilowatt hours in 1970–71 to 398 billion kwh by 1990–91 (an average annual growth rate of 10.5 percent), with 55 percent of electricity generated in 1991 going to industrial uses and over 10 percent to irrigation pumpsets (Parikh [1976], 54). This consumption was to be supplied by an installed capacity of 92.3 gigawatts, of which coal-fired thermal plants were to supply 50.7 GW and hydro-electric plants 33 GW. Diesel and oil-fired generating plants were to be completely phased out, but a rapidly growing nuclear sector would supply 8.6 GW of capacity (Parikh [1976], 54).

Expanding the output of coal for power plants implied shifting from underground to open-pit mining of non-coking coal reserves, investing in coal washeries, creating transmission facilities to accommodate pitmouth power plants and railway capacity to transport coal. Hydroelectric power generation was thought to entail substantial cost advantages, and the ultimate potential capacity was optimistically estimated at 80 to 100 GW, with few qualifications on account of potential ecological or social constraints. India's limited uranium reserves were thought adequate to support up to 10 GW of capacity in first generation plants, with the ultimate potential to use recycled plutonium in fast breeder reactors to support 600 to 1,000 GW of capacity. This assessment gave little attention to nuclear waste management, safety, or siting issues. On the basis of information available in the early 1970s, without the experience of actual nuclear installations to evaluate, the *Second India Study* concluded that nuclear energy was economically justified for India. Renewable energy sources, such as wind and solar, were considered uneconomical through the end of the century despite falling cost trajectories. In short, the *Second India Study* envisaged an enormous expansion in the capacity to utilize commercial fuels (Parikh [1976], 51).

B. Actual Rural Energy Developments

Although with the benefit of hindsight some obvious flaws appear in this technological vision, the main divergences with actual developments stem from unforeseen institutional and policy problems. In the rural areas, the use of collected biomass fuels has continued to grow because the availability of alternative sources has not increased nearly to the extent the *Second India Study* envisaged. Although rural electrification has spread rapidly to cover 84 percent of India's villages by 1991 and energized nearly 9 million pumpsets—a significant achievement—still only about 27 percent of rural households are connected (Pachauri, 4.3). Despite partial compensation from the central government's Rural Electrifi-

cation Corporation, the state electricity boards are losing large sums on rural electrification because tariffs cover only one seventh of supply costs on average. During the 1970s and 1980s most of these state boards actually lowered tariffs for agriculture in real terms and adopted flat rates per installed horsepower instead of tariffs based on metered energy use, working against end-use efficiencies in pumping (Pachauri, 4.8). As a result, although agriculture's share of the total electricity consumption has risen dramatically from 9 percent in 1970–71 to 25 percent twenty years later, financial losses have risen too (Pachauri, 8.7).

Biogas plants have also not been adopted nearly to the extent envisaged. Of the 12 million households that the *Second India Study* estimated would be able to support a family installation, ap-

Table 3. Rural Energy Consumption Pattern (Percent)

State	Kerosene	Total Commercial	Logs, Twigs, & Charcoal	Crop Waste	Dung	Total Non-Commercial
Andhra Pradesh	8.7	10.2	58.7	10.4	8.4	89.5
Assam	9.7	10.5	69.4	20.1	0.0	89.5
Bihar	3.7	7.8	31.2	19.9	41.1	92.2
Gujarat	26.3	32.7	54.3	2.7	14.7	66.7
Haryana	4.2	9.4	19.4	27.3	43.6	90.6
Himachal Pradesh	7.4	12.1	88.1	0.4	0.7	88.9
Jammu/Kashmir	5.9	9.7	64.4	3.0	22.9	90.3
Karnataka	6.5	9.3	74.0	14.7	1.6	90.3
Kerala	7.2	10.9	59.6	29.5	0.0	89.1
Madhya Pradesh	4.1	4.8	56.2	12.3	26.8	95.3
Maharashtra	14.6	19.5	62.1	4.3	13.7	80.1
Meghalaya	6.1	6.7	77.8	15.5	0.0	93.3
Orissa	3.6	5.7	61.3	9.6	23.4	87.2
Punjab	2.8	3.7	70.5	4.0	21.7	87.2
Rajasthan	9.2	12.7	66.4	13.4	7.4	96.2
Tamil Nadu	3.6	4.6	35.0	19.0	32.4	87.2
West Bengal	7.0	21.4	25.1	38.9	14.6	86.4
Delhi	4.6	43.4	28.1	13.6	14.7	78.6
ALL INDIA	7.1	10.8	51.6	16.3	21.1	89.0

Source: GOI, Planning Commission (1992); Pachauri (1994).

proximately 1.3 million had one by 1990–1 (Pachauri, 6.5). Only about 1,000 community plants were in existence to serve the remaining rural population. Many villages haven't been able to cooperate in running community facilities and distributing the outputs. Moreover, although bio-gas plants are potentially economical for their operators, even without taking environmental benefits into account, the central government created highly subsidized promotional credit and construction programs to accelerate diffusion. This approach inadvertently discouraged private entrepreneurs from entering the industry, although they might have built better service and distribution networks and improved design and construction methods. At the same time, performance standards among government contractors have been at best inconsistent. Surveys have shown that only two-thirds of installed plants were functioning in 1991, the rest out of commission because of faulty construction or maintenance (Pachauri, 6.5). The national program to promote the use of improved cookstoves has had a similar experience. The user subsidy amounts to 80 to 90 percent of the cost, and the program has operated in a top-down, target-oriented way. Through 1992, almost 13 million stoves have been installed, but far fewer are in operation and the realized energy savings are less than anticipated (Pachauri, 6.6). Over the long term, relying on government programs rather than private markets to diffuse economically attractive technologies has probably retarded, rather than advanced, their rate of diffusion.

Problems of sustaining communal use of forests for fuel and fodder have not been resolved, despite government efforts. On most village commons and state forests, effective mechanisms to limit harvesting to sustainable levels or to enlist widespread participation in reforestation and conservation efforts have been lacking—the so-called tragedy of the commons. Moreover, state forestry agencies have traditionally been more oriented to revenue-yielding commercial production than to meeting the needs of the rural poor (Agarwal [1993], 4–5). Government development programs have attempted fuelwood production schemes in deficit districts, social forestry schemes, and par-

In the late 1980s, firewood consumption was still six times the recorded production from forest areas. Farm forestry programs have expanded on private lands, but the harvested wood has typically been sold as more valuable poles or pulpwood and has been beyond the means of the poor.

ticipatory reforestation programs under the National Wastelands Development Board. Cumulatively, 18 million ha. have been reforested under these programs, with an estimated success rate of about 30 percent and average yields of 3.7 tons/ha/year (Pachauri, 5.5). Often, however, grazing pressures and competition prevented past harvest regeneration from other species. Fast growing and hardy species, such as *Prosopis juliflora*, (mesquite), may improve on past performance. Social forestry models successfully tested and now adopted in 14 states show that performance also improves when local communities are involved at each stage. Recent legislative changes requiring that local governments be popularly elected and requiring state forestry agencies to share management responsibilities with them are steps in this direction. However, to date, "All these efforts could not reduce the gap between consumption and availability…in view of the lack of funds for implementation, and also because of the tremendous increase in human as well as livestock populations" (Pachauri, 5.3). In the late 1980s, firewood consumption was still six times the recorded production from forest areas. Farm forestry programs have expanded on private lands, but the harvested wood has typically been sold as more valuable poles or pulpwood and has been beyond the means of the poor.

So the rural energy deficit and use of biomass fuels have continued or even increased since the

Second India Study was completed. Although estimates of current consumption vary widely, the range strongly indicates that burning of dung, residues, and firewood in rural areas has increased (Parikh [1976], Table 2.1; Pachauri, Table 11.2). Surveys indicate that firewood continues to be the preferred biomass fuel where it's available, but crop residues and dung are heavily used in dry and deforested regions—many of which already lack soil organic matter.

Deforestation averaged 339,000 hectares per year during the 1980s, 0.6 percent of the remaining stock annually (World Resources Institute, Table 19.1; p. 306). Because stocks are depleted, women and girls, the main fuel collectors, must spend more and more time bringing fuel from greater distances. On the plains of Madhya Pradesh or the hilly areas of Haryana, for example, women must make two or three trips per week for firewood, covering 4–5 km each time—a total time commitment of 20 hours per week or more. As discussed above, this time commitment and fuelwood shortages combine to reduce household income. Even nutrition suffers as fewer cooked meals are possible. Women also suffer the effects of high particulate and carbon monoxide concentrations from cooking fires on traditional stoves in poorly ventilated dwellings, and suffer significantly higher rates of chronic bronchitis than do women who use non-biomass fuels.

In addition, the increase in the numbers of urban poor living in slums has kept urban demand for firewood growing. Rising prices have allowed firewood, harvested mostly from state and communal woodlands, to be trucked from ever greater distances around major cities (Bowonder, *Air Pollution*, 23). Soft coal briquettes have not been marketed successfully as a substitute for cooking fuel because their prices, availability, and burning qualities have been unattractive.

C. Petroleum Demand and Supply

Efforts to slow growth in the consumption of petroleum fuels succeeded during the 1970s and early 1980s largely because energy prices were high and economic growth slow (Bowonder, *Air Pollution*, 22). But, during the 1980s, when those conditions were reversed, consumption accelerated. Over the entire period, the consumption of petroleum products increased at an average annual rate of 6.5 percent. With the exception of aircraft fuel and light diesel oil, consumption of petroleum products has outpaced *Second India Study* projections, despite substantial efforts to replace oil with coal, electricity, and natural gas in industrial uses (Pachauri, Table 1.3). The explanation lies in transportation sector developments quite contrary to the solutions proposed in the *Second India Study*.

Despite the diseconomies the *Second India Study* foresaw, the period 1971–91 saw road transport rapidly replacing railways, both for freight and passenger traffic. Freight movement by road increased 8.2 percent annually, compared to 3.4 percent for railroads (Pachauri, 9.1). By 1991, most freight moved by road, even over distances that gave railways a theoretical cost advantage. Trucking's competitive advantage stemmed from its greater reliability, flexibility, and convenience. Over much of the period, capacity bottlenecks, backward technologies, and personnel and managerial problems kept public sector railways from maintaining, let alone increasing, their position as commodity carriers. The electrification program foreseen in the *Second India Study* to reduce diesel use in railroads is still incomplete (Pachauri, 9.4).

Even more dramatic has been the falling share of urban mass transit. Over the period 1970–91, the number of motorscooters and motorcycles on the road grew 17 percent per year, compared to 7 percent for cars and jeeps, and 6 percent for buses, even though buses are potentially far more efficient (Pachauri, 9.2). Per million passenger miles, cars use 4.9 times and two-wheelers 2.6 times the energy as buses, occupy 38.5 and 54 times the road space, cost 9.5 and 3.1 times as much to operate, and emit 5.7 and 3.1 times the air pollutants. Although people in all developing countries have demonstrated a strong demand for personal vehicles, public transportation in

India has also been held back by underinvestment and poor maintenance and service. One of the principal reasons, as with railways, has been inadequate internal generation of operating and investment funds. Fares that have been kept low for political and equity reasons have, in most cases, not even covered operating costs let alone an investment budget for expansion. Moreover, minimizing vehicular traffic through urban planning, as envisaged in the *Second India Study*, hasn't worked at all (Pachauri, 9.7). Instead of compact, medium-sized cities, rent controls and restrictions on urban land development has discouraged high density construction downtown in many cities and stimulated suburban developments. Consequently, private investment in motor vehicles has dominated the transportation sector, outpacing capacity increases in congested urban roads, as well as in overcrowded urban mass transit. The share of petroleum among transportation fuels has not fallen, but actually risen substantially from 67 percent in 1970–71 to 91 percent in 1990 (Pachauri, 9.3). At the same time, congestion, urban air pollution, and road accidents have become increasingly severe problems. *(See Figure 24.)*

These difficulties in reducing petroleum use have led to serious balance of payments problems, as the *Second India Study* foresaw. India's oil import burden would have been much more serious had the *Second India Study*'s over-optimism regarding substitution possibilities not been balanced by undue pessimism about India's oil and gas resources. When that study was done, less than 10 percent of India's potential hydrocarbon-bearing territory had been explored, and only preliminary indications of offshore resources (in particular, in the "Bombay High") had come to light (Pachauri, 3.2, 3.7). After the oil price shocks of the 1970s, the Indian government dramatically increased its own exploration efforts and invited private sector participation. These efforts have successfully discovered and developed substantially greater potential oil and gas resources. Despite the past 20 years' production, proven re-

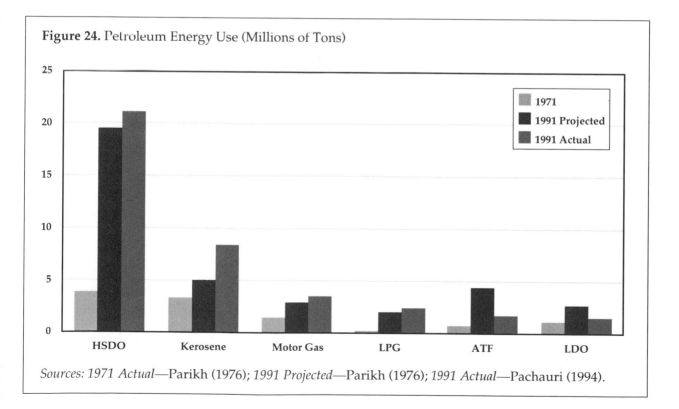

Figure 24. Petroleum Energy Use (Millions of Tons)

Sources: 1971 Actual—Parikh (1976); 1991 Projected—Parikh (1976); 1991 Actual—Pachauri (1994).

*India's oil import burden would have been much more serious had the **Second India Study's** over-optimism regarding substitution possibilities not been balanced by undue pessimism about India's oil and gas resources.*

serves of oil in 1990–91 are seven times higher than in 1970–71 and those of natural gas ten times higher (Pachauri, 9.3). As in many other countries, the reserve-production ratio has not fallen despite rapid production growth (Pachauri, 3.7; Bowonder, *Energy*, 17).

In the case of natural gas, however, the lingering perception that resources were meager has retarded the investments needed to develop markets and downstream uses for the gas that has been found (Parikh & Parikh, 261). The government has controlled prices and allocated production almost exclusively to fertilizer and petrochemical plants. Despite severe power shortages and the advantages of easily constructed gas turbine power plants, distribution networks and potential industrial fuel markets have not been encouraged. Consequently, substantial excess production capacity emerged in some basins. In addition, enormous amounts of gas have been flared (Pachauri, 3.3). Since 1980, for lack of collection and distribution facilities, 20 billion cubic meters of natural gas have been flared just in the Bombay High offshore production area, equivalent to 18 million tons of oil worth $2.5 billion. Only in recent years has the policy of flaring been reversed (Parikh & Parikh, 260–61).

D. Electric Power

Ironically, the oil and gas sector, in which resource endowments were considered limited, has exceeded projected capacity increases; the coal

and electricity sectors, in which India's resources were considered ample, have fallen far short. Hydroelectricity capacity, considered especially attractive for peaking power, was little more than one-half the *Second India Study* forecast in 1990–91, and its share in total installed power capacity has fallen steadily from 43 percent in 1970–71 to 28 percent in 1990–91 (Pachauri, 4.5). *(See Figure 25.)* The ecological issues of stream and watershed disruption voiced by environmental groups, and the problems in resettling large numbers of villages emphasized by social activists have caused a slowdown in hydroelectricity development. These issues have become far more prominent as time passed. The other impediments were mostly the more prosaic ones of inter-state water sharing disputes, delays in site acquisition and construction, rising costs and inadequate funding.

Growth in thermal power capacity, although very substantial, also lagged behind *Second India Study* forecasts. Nonetheless, the concentration of large coal-fired power stations at pitmouth in the coalmining regions of Bengal and Bihar has led to serious local environmental impacts, including acid rain and ash accumulations. The lag in capacity generation stems from institutional and policy problems, not from any shortage of energy resources. Overstaffing and other excessive costs in state electricity boards combined with controlled electricity tariffs far below long-run marginal costs or even average costs have left the SEBs without enough internal funds for investment (Parikh & Parikh, 259). The gap between average costs and returns has widened from Rs 0.04 per kwh generated in 1974–75 to Rs. 0.24 in 1990–91 (Pachauri, 4.8). The Central Government has stepped in with financial support, but hasn't been willing or able to fill the gap entirely. Power availability has been further curtailed by high transmission losses and distribution, which have remained above 20 percent—higher than in 1970–71.

For a number of reasons, plant and system-wide load factors have also declined over the past 20 years. State Electricity Boards operate a large number of small plants in poor condition and

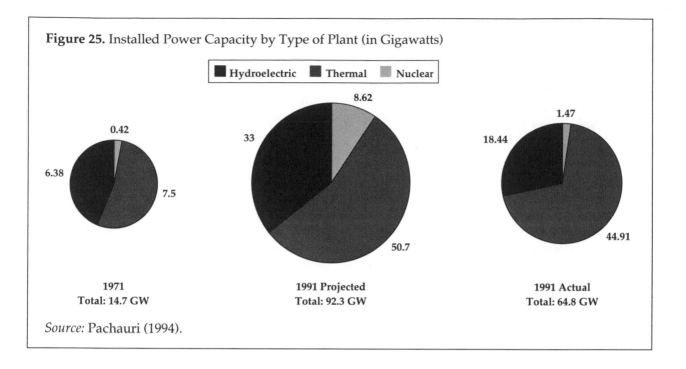

Figure 25. Installed Power Capacity by Type of Plant (in Gigawatts)

■ Hydroelectric ■ Thermal ▨ Nuclear

1971
Total: 14.7 GW

0.42
6.38
7.5

1991 Projected
Total: 92.3 GW

8.62
33
50.7

1991 Actual
Total: 64.8 GW

1.47
18.44
44.91

Source: Pachauri (1994).

can't renovate and modernize them. The SEB's are not fully connected in transmission grids, and even where they are, do not integrate their power plant operations to maximize availability (Parikh & Parikh, 259). Also relevant, the average grade of coal received at thermal power plants has declined, from 4,600 kcal/kg in 1975 to 3,800–4,100 in 1985–86, adversely affecting boiler efficiency, maintenance, particulate control and ash handling (Pachauri, 4.7). This is partly an inevitable consequence of the large-scale shift to open-pit mining of coal seams interspersed with rock, but also in part the result of poor quality control by the public monopoly that was formed in the early 1970s to take over coal production, and of inadequate investment in coal washeries, despite their demonstrated returns.

These problems have led to electricity shortfalls in many states during the late 1970s and 1980s, estimated currently for the entire country at 8.5 percent of total electricity generated and 17.5 percent at peak periods (Pachauri, 4.1). Brownouts, voltage fluctuations, and supply interruptions have been common. The resulting substantial production losses have prompted

many industries to install their own backup diesel-fired capacity and persuaded farmers to buy backup diesel-powered pumps. Even though these problems and the private sector's reactions to them have substantially boosted national energy costs, until quite recently India avoided using a market approach to reduce excess demand by raising average and peak period tariffs.

These energy shortages would have been much greater had Indian development been as energy intensive as the *Second India Study* envisaged it would be. The overall energy efficiency of the economy has improved with the shift toward modern fuels since traditional biomass fuels are both converted and used very inefficiently. In addition, the *Second India Study* underestimated the extent to which technological improvements within industries would reduce energy demands, even without strong conservation policies and price signals. For this reason, while consumption of petroleum products has increased in line with projections, the use of electricity and, especially, coal was greatly overestimated. Since most of India's coal is used for power generation, the two overestimates are inter-linked, of course. (*See Fig-*

ure 26.) But, the industrial sector, which consumes about half of India's commercial energy, became 28 percent less energy intensive between 1972 and 1988 and consumes far less energy than expected (Pachauri, 7.1). *(See Figure 27.)*

The steel industry, for example, has largely converted from open hearth to electric arc furnaces, with a substantial gain in efficiency. Cement plants have almost completely replaced the wet process with dry process technology, with at least a 20 percent energy savings. In the fertilizer industry, with the construction of new natural gas feedstock plants, energy consumption per ton of ammonia has fallen 17 percent since 1970 (Pachauri, 7.1). Many industries have switched to higher efficiency electric motors and improved design boilers. Overall, the energy efficiency of the manufacturing sector improved by 60 percent between 1974 and 1986. Since then, greater openness to world technological developments and heightened competitive pressures have probably maintained or increased the rate of improvement. Overall improvement would have been even greater, had not relatively energy-intensive industries, such as chemicals and metals, grown faster than industry as a whole.

Despite these gains, most Indian industries still use considerably more energy per unit of output than their equivalents in other countries do. Government of India studies and commissions have found that the scope for cost-effective energy savings is large, at least 25 percent in industry and

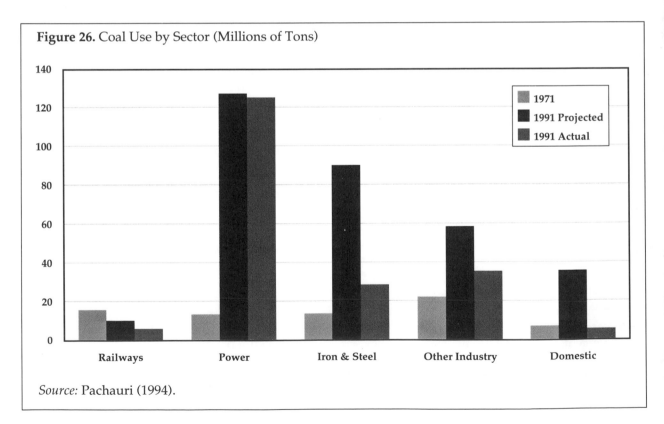

Figure 26. Coal Use by Sector (Millions of Tons)

Source: Pachauri (1994).

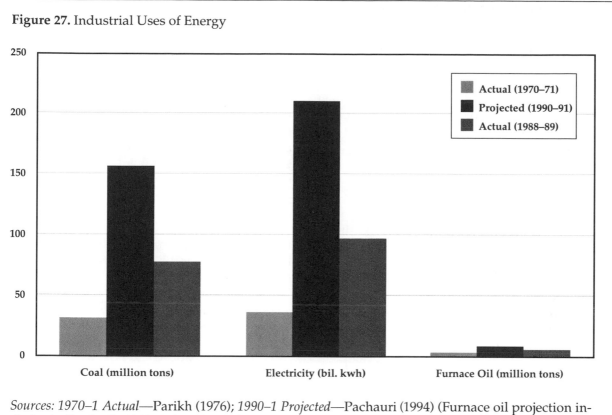

Figure 27. Industrial Uses of Energy

Legend:
- Actual (1970–71)
- Projected (1990–91)
- Actual (1988–89)

Categories (x-axis): Coal (million tons), Electricity (bil. kwh), Furnace Oil (million tons)

Sources: 1970–1 Actual—Parikh (1976); *1990–1 Projected*—Pachauri (1994) (Furnace oil projection includes boiler fuel); *1988–9 Actual*—Pachauri (1994).

close to this figure in other sectors. Several special government programs were initiated to promote energy savings, including credit schemes and fiscal incentives, but they were "sporadic, ad-hoc and uncoordinated" so their impact has been marginal (Pachauri, 12.2). Energy pricing policies, especially in agriculture but more generally with respect to coal, electricity, and some petroleum products, have not been used to foster energy conservation (Pachauri, 12.3).

Even though India's per capita use of commercial fuels remains much lower than the industrial countries', the environmental impacts are evident: high levels of urban air pollution, severe land and water degradation in coal mining regions, and ecological and social disruptions from multipurpose hydro projects. Pollution abatement equipment is mandatory on major new in-

vestments, but constraints have kept these policies from being fully implemented. Far less progress has been made in reducing the environmental impacts of existing factories since many use obsolete technologies and many—especially small and medium-sized plants—have limited financial, technical, and managerial resources. Nor do state pollution control boards have adequate capacities for monitoring and enforcement (Bowonder, *Environmental Regulations*, 4).

Since the *Second India Study* was carried out, the greenhouse issue has emerged as a completely new potential environmental factor affecting India's energy sector and, potentially, the overall economy. In discussing the need to develop coal resources, the *Second India Study* made no mention of potential climate change as a possible constraint. The issue became increasingly salient during the 1980s, and an international treaty to control greenhouse gases has been negotiated and has entered into force. As the world's fifth or sixth largest emitter of greenhouse gas, with heavy reliance on coal—a carbon-rich fuel—India now must decide how best to respond (Parikh & Gokarn [1992], 3). In the short-term, the obvious options include policies to improve energy efficiency, to shift toward natural gas and renewable energy sources, and to develop clean coal technologies.

India has still to address outstanding institutional and policy issues as well. In order to finance the heavy investment requirements of the energy sector and to improve efficiency, a framework must be created to attract private investment and to allow public sector energy enterprises to behave more like commercial enterprises, without sacrificing social objectives. Among other things, this will require substantial revision of energy prices and the price-setting mechanism. Mechanisms are still to be developed that will promote integrated development and management of India's energy resources, including greater attention to efficiency in energy end uses.

In summary, India has rapidly developed its energy resources over the past two decades in response to the demands of population and economic growth. However, institutional and policy constraints have impeded the solution of India's energy problems. In rural areas, the problems of managing community resources and the difficulty of developing markets for non-traditional energy devices among dispersed low-income households have been constraining. In the urban-industrial economy, managing India's energy resources and providing appropriate economic incentives have been the principal challenges. Throughout the period, new discoveries and technologies, new developments in international energy markets, and new environmental challenges have emerged that the *Second India Study* did not and probably could not have foreseen.

VIII. Industry

Industrial growth in India over the past twenty years has made a disappointingly small contribution to poverty alleviation, but a relatively large contribution to environmental degradation. In the two decades as a whole, industrial output grew more slowly than in other developing Asian economies and didn't meet India's own growth targets. Industrial employment grew more slowly still, creating relatively few of the jobs needed to occupy rural outmigrants and better-educated labor force entrants. Structural shifts toward more polluting industrial sectors, the persistence of relatively backward industrial technologies, and weakly applied environmental regulations have combined to raise the pollution intensity of Indian industry. The health of susceptible workers and low income urban residents has been affected. However, the Bhopal accident in 1984 and other unmistakable evidence of pollution also created the political impulse to strengthen environmental laws and regulations during the 1980s.

Also, during the 1980s, other policy changes began to improve the industrial situation. Expansionary fiscal measures increased consumer demand at a faster rate. Infrastructure investments broke up some transport and power bottlenecks. Relaxing government licensing requirements for industrial investments and imports of industrial inputs increased competition and permitted output to increase in response to demand. The diversified base of industrial capacity established in the 1960s and 1970s began to be used more fully. These changes increased industrial growth and productivity. Yet, employment growth in organized industry continued to lag as redundant workers were absorbed and as firms sought to avoid taking on the obligations of increased staff.

A. Indian Industrial Policy at the Time of the *Second India Study*

India's nationalist leaders conceived what would become its industrialization strategy as far back as the 1930s, marrying an admiration for the Soviet Union's rapid industrial growth with pessimism about the future prospects for world trade, which had all but collapsed in the Great Depression. The strategy of import substitution and direct government control over industry was born during the crisis years of WWII, when trade with England was cut off. It was nurtured during the early years of independence, when both government and business agreed that fledgling Indian industries needed protection and public sector support (Mohan [1992]). It was articulated in the first Five-year plan, which postulated that government's intervention and involvement were needed to direct investments into the production of import-substituting capital goods and industrial intermediates while holding down the growth of consumer demand to raise the rate of national savings. Spurred by large public investments in heavy industry and diverse private investments behind high protective barriers, industrial growth in the 1950s and early 1960s was rapid until limited by balance of payments crises and chronic foreign exchange shortages.

By the late 1960s or early 1970s, when the *Second India Study* was undertaken, this industrialization strategy had run out of steam. Public sector enterprises in steel, heavy equipment, and basic chemicals were operating at low rates of capacity utilization and profitability, because of supply bottlenecks, demand shortfalls, and managerial problems. Even though typically overstaffed and highly protected, these capital-intensive public sector industries were generating few new jobs and low returns on public funds invested in them.

In the private sector, the slow growth in per capita incomes in the 1960s fundamentally constrained the growth of demand for manufactured goods. High prices, maintained by tariffs and strict import quotas, as well as domestic excises, discouraged "inessential" consumption and further restricted demand. Because Indian planners considered competitive investments wasteful, industrial licensing created virtual monopoly conditions for many local producers, also pushing up prices. In addition, many staple manufactured goods were "reserved" for small-scale and cottage industries, and factory production was prohibited.

Indian industry was no less constrained on the supply side. Pervasive government controls over new investments, industrial finance, imports of capital goods and components, and joint venture or technology licensing agreements with foreign collaborators handcuffed domestic entrepreneurs. Price controls and the administrative rationing systems they necessitated created persistent shortages of power and rail transportation and of coal, steel, and other basic industrial raw materials. The loss of export competitiveness, the overvaluation of the rupee, and the pull of the sheltered domestic market created chronic shortages of foreign exchange, so imports of industrial intermediates and materials had to be strictly controlled.

In this climate, the growth of industrial output slowed from an average of 7 percent per year in the 1950s to 5 percent in the 1960s—well below the target growth rates Indian planners adopted during those periods. More tellingly, this was only one third to one half the growth rates being racked up by other Asian developing countries, such as Thailand and Korea, that had adopted outward oriented, market-driven industrialization policies. India's share of world exports fell steadily from 2.0 percent in 1950 to only 0.65 percent in 1970 (Ahluwalia [1991]). Traditional exports such as cotton and jute textiles lost market share, and new manufacturing export industries that fueled rapid growth in other countries bypassed India almost completely.

If industrial output grew slowly, employment fared even worse, increasing at only about half the rate as industrial production. Government policy restricted private investment in light industries manufacturing consumer products, while public sector funds were invested in heavy equipment and industrial materials industries. The inward-looking trade regime discouraged the potentially rapid growth of labor-intensive export industries. In addition, industrial incentives rewarded the installation of new capacity and discouraged hiring of new workers: cheap credits and tax advantages were linked to investment rather than to additional output or employment. Rationed imports and raw materials were allocated according to plant capacity. Moreover, the licensing of investments usually prevented additional investment once "sufficient" capacity had been installed, so private firms could create barriers to entry and monopoly positions if they could build plant capacity ahead of demand. At the same time, labor legislation pushed wage costs far above those in non-factory sectors by supporting union wage demands, mandating fringe benefits, and making it virtually impossible to remove redundant workers or rationalize the workforce. Labor policy was oriented far more to protecting existing jobs than to creating new ones (World Bank [1990]).

These policies had serious consequences. While employment grew by about 3 percent yearly over the 1960s, the capital-labor ratio in Indian industry doubled (Ahluwalia, 40, 51). The increase in factory employment was actually *slower* than the increase in the urban labor force. Organized industry was not helping to reduce the enormous burden of rural underemployment, nor even preventing an increase in urban poverty.

B. The *Second India Study's* Alternative Vision and its Fate

In this context, the *Second India Study* offered an alternative pathway for industrial development over the rest of the century. Its scenarios suggested that continuing with the past strategy would not generate enough employment to reduce poverty. As an alternative, it suggested redirecting investment into more labor-intensive industries—which it roughly equated (not entirely accurately) with consumer goods industries. While the policy implications of this alternative were not spelled out in detail, the *Second India Study* authors recognized that this alternative implied relaxing the import-substitution imperative, exporting more of the country's industrial output, and hence, paying more attention to the mandates of comparative advantage and external market forces (Ezekiel [1975]). This prescription echoed a substantial body of opinion at this time (Bhagwati & Desai [1970]).

During the 1970s, Indian policy-makers for the most part resisted these suggestions. As a result, virtually the same alignment of industrial licensing, import controls, and public sector domination of heavy industries continued for another decade. Performance plateaued. Industrial output and value added grew only about 4 percent per year over the decade. Capital intensity increased by about another 40 percent by 1980. Productivity in the overall use of labor and capital continued to decline. *(See Figure 28.)* India's share in export markets fell even further, from 0.65 percent in 1970 to 0.42 percent in 1980. The overall return on capital invested in public sector industries in that year was negative, even though the petroleum sector earned profits during the oil crisis. Employment showed no faster increase. As in the 1960s, industrialization offered little escape to the increasing numbers of urban poor and totally

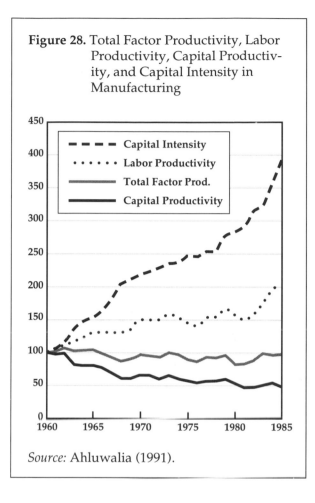

Figure 28. Total Factor Productivity, Labor Productivity, Capital Productivity, and Capital Intensity in Manufacturing

Source: Ahluwalia (1991).

failed to provide the new jobs that could cut into massive rural underemployment.

Indian planners, politicians and top civil servants, who resisted recommendations for change throughout this period, had never been burdened with excessive humility. They never doubted their ability to discern the desirable pattern of investment, nor their ability to force the economy's resources in those directions. In fact, in the end, they were able to do neither. They grossly overestimated the benefits of investing in steel, industrial machinery, and other heavy industries. They totally missed the advantages of integrating into global markets and the coming dominance of information technologies. The "commanding heights" of the economy to which they aspired sank under the weight of economic inefficiency and political interference—veritable sinkholes into which public finances disappeared.

Further, not only were they unable to control the flow of private investment, they couldn't even control their own bureaucracies. Licensing and import controls created huge monopoly rents for investors in "inessential" industries, into which money inexorably seeped. Price controls limited profits in so-called "basic" industries, so private investors shunned them. And throughout, the morass of permits and regulations created such opportunities for graft that corruption and special interests ultimately became the only support for the "Licensing Raj," keeping it in place long after its economic rationale had crumbled.

The need for trade protection became a self-fulfilling prophecy. Introduced to shelter "infant industries" behind tariff and quota barriers, it fostered industries with inadequate plant sizes, obsolete technologies, inferior quality products, inflated payrolls, and mediocre management.

The need for trade protection became a self-fulfilling prophecy. Introduced to shelter "infant industries" behind tariff and quota barriers, it fostered industries with inadequate plant sizes, obsolete technologies, inferior quality products, inflated payrolls, and mediocre management. Not only could such enterprises not compete internationally, all other Indian firms forced to buy their products for no better reason than their "indigenous availability" were burdened with shoddy, high-priced components and equipment—a major disadvantage in world competition. Shut out of world markets, much of Indian industry was consigned to trade with USSR and Eastern Europe for their equally inferior merchandise under bilateral trade arrangements.

Because Indian industry was unable—and given the sheltered domestic market—largely unwilling to develop export markets, and because world demand for such traditional agricultural exports as tea and jute grew only slowly, India wrestled with chronic balance of payments deficits. Shortages of foreign exchange and weakness in the rupee reinforced the perceived need to protect the economy against imports—another self-fulfilling prophecy.

Import substitution drove the economy into highly capital-intensive industries in which India had less and less comparative advantage. Meanwhile, by developing precisely those sectors of relatively labor-intensive manufacturing from which India had banished itself, the East and Southeast Asian economies were enjoying phenomenal rates of export and industrial growth. While those economies found various forms of foreign collaboration a way of increasing access to foreign technology, designs, distribution networks and markets, India pursued a policy of self-sufficiency that was highly restrictive of—and sometimes outrightly hostile to—foreign investment. Although intended to foster domestic technology and entrepreneurs, the cost was slower diffusion and adaptation of technological innovations originating elsewhere.

C. Industry's Environmental Impacts

This policy orientation has contributed to the industry's environmental impacts, along with structural changes and weak implementation of pollution controls. The share of highly polluting industries, especially those that generate hazardous and toxic wastes, has increased substantially. These include electricity, chemicals and petroleum refining, basic metals, non-metallic minerals, paper, and leather industries, whose share in industrial value added rose from 45 to 52 percent between 1975 and 1989 (Bowonder & Rao, 12). Not only are the wastes from these industries

Table 4. Status of Pollution Control in Identified Polluting Industries

Industry and Particulars of Compliance	Number of Plants	Percent of Total
OIL INDUSTRY	12	
Plants complying with effluent and emission standards	6	50
FERTILIZER INDUSTRY	110	
Plants complying with emission standards only	49	44.5
THERMAL POWER PLANTS	70	
Plants complying with emission standards	25	35.7
Plants complying with the standards for ashpond effluents	33	47
INTEGRATED IRON AND STEEL PLANTS	7	
Plants partially complying with effluent and emission standards	6	85.7
Plants not complying with emission standards	1	14.3
CEMENT INDUSTRY	94	
Plants complying with emission standards	62	66
PULP AND PAPER INDUSTRY	336	
Plants having fully operational ETPs	118	35.1
Plants having partially operational ETPs	49	14.6
SUGAR INDUSTRY	365	
Plants having fully operational ETPs	180	49.3
Plants having partially operational ETPs	31	8.5
DISTILLERY INDUSTRY	176	
Plants having fully operational ETPs	74	42
Plants having partially operational ETPs	32	18.2

Note: ETP means effluent treatment plant.
Source: Bowonder and Rao (1994).

especially hazardous to health, they have typically been dumped on fallow or public lands without any proper safeguards, thus making their way into water bodies or the air (Kirloskar Consultants [1991]). Proper facilities for treating and permanently disposing of the growing volume of hazardous wastes have not been available. Hundreds of thousands of tons of hazardous wastes improperly discarded threaten the present generation's health and impose environmental and economic burdens on future generations.

Compliance with emissions standards and pollution control standards has been slow, especially in older establishments, financially weak firms, and in small-scale enterprises. In all of these, there are often financial, technological, or managerial constraints to compliance. In major industries, even in 1991, fewer than half the operating plants were in full compliance with emissions standards or had fully operational effluent-treatment plants.

Moreover, despite efforts to disperse industry around the country, production remains highly concentrated, so pollution is concentrated too. Four states—Gujarat, Uttar Pradesh, Maharashtra, and Tamil Nadu—accounted for 52 percent of industrial production in 1988–89, and 57 percent of new investments in pollution-intensive rubber, chemicals, and petrochemicals industries.

One population severely at risk is the industrial workforce itself. The combination of obsolete technology and lax pollution controls typically leads to high exposure levels and inadequate protection of factory workers. Field studies from the 1970s and 1980s found disturbingly high occurrences of occupational diseases in various industries. For example, 29 percent of cotton mill workers in one study showed symptoms of byssinosis, 16 percent of workers in ceramics factories in another study had silicosis, 58 percent of workers in pesticide factories showed symptoms of poisoning in a third study, and so on. Occupational health problems are especially severe in such industries as leather tanning, where small-scale firms using primitive technologies and toxic materials predominate (IGIDR [1993]).

Industrial pollution also affects the general population. Precise epidemiological linkages are hard to establish, because low income urban populations are exposed to a variety of environmental assaults: unsafe drinking water, vehicular exhausts, and cookstove fumes, for example. They are also malnourished and burdened with high levels of communicable and chronic diseases. Industrial pollution acts synergistically with other health problems in these highly vulnerable populations. Poverty, lack of access to adequate preventive and curative health care, and exposure to pollution interact in industrial slum areas.

In the three highly industrialized states of Tamil Nadu, Gujarat, and Maharashtra, per capita incomes are above the national average.

Yet, deaths in urban areas from respiratory and water-borne diseases are disproportionately high. In 1988, these three states held 20.6 percent of India's population, but accounted for 40 percent of all fatalities from waterborne diseases and 48 percent of total deaths from respiratory diseases. Although rates of urban and rural poverty have declined in all three states, their combined share of total deaths from respiratory diseases rose from 39 to 48 percent between 1970 and 1988, and their share in waterborne diseases rose from 38 to 40 percent. Moreover, despite higher per capita incomes and better health facilities in urban areas, these three states' share in urban deaths from these diseases was higher than their share in rural deaths from the same environmentally related diseases. (See Figures 29 and 30.)

Moreover, urban death rates within these three states are higher in districts where industries are concentrated than in districts where there are few

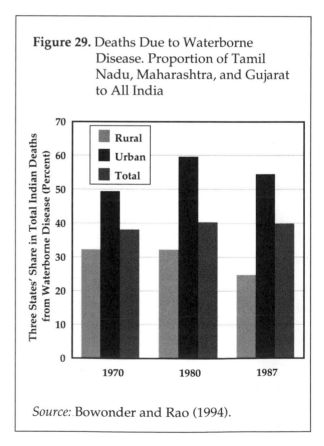

Figure 29. Deaths Due to Waterborne Disease. Proportion of Tamil Nadu, Maharashtra, and Gujarat to All India

Source: Bowonder and Rao (1994).

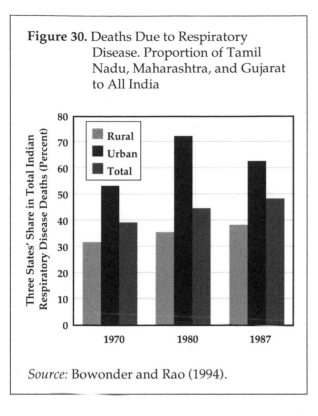

Figure 30. Deaths Due to Respiratory Disease. Proportion of Tamil Nadu, Maharashtra, and Gujarat to All India

Source: Bowonder and Rao (1994).

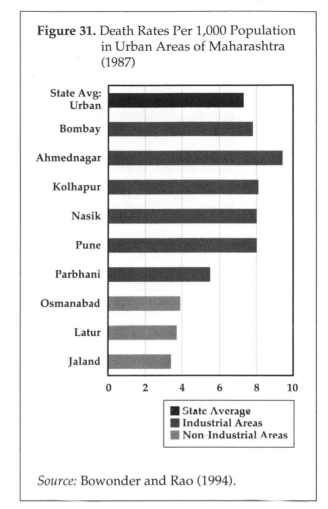

Figure 31. Death Rates Per 1,000 Population in Urban Areas of Maharashtra (1987)

Source: Bowonder and Rao (1994).

industries, even though per capita incomes are lower where industry is sparse. *(See Figures 31, 32 and 33.)* Of course, from an epidemiological perspective, these data are extremely crude and call for more detailed and sophisticated investigation. However, the magnitudes of the differentials certainly suggest the synergistic role of industrial pollution in compounding the health problems of low-income populations.

The Bhopal accident in 1984 stimulated new measures to coordinate environmental regula-

Urban death rates are higher in districts where industries are concentrated than in districts where there are few industries, even though per capita incomes are lower where industry is sparse.

tions affecting industries and to strengthen implementation. A comprehensive Environmental Protection Act in 1986 brought hazardous wastes under regulation, sanctioned citizen initiated action against violators, and put non-complying firms at risk of shutdowns and even criminal proceedings against management. While these more stringent laws and subsequent implementing measures have prompted many firms to install pollution control facilities on an agreed compliance schedule, and have resulted in the closure of some highly polluting plants, they have had their limitations as well. The threat of closure and criminal prosecution and the absence of more moderate administrative or economic penalties has naturally resulted in a surge of litigation, much of which languishes in the judicial system.

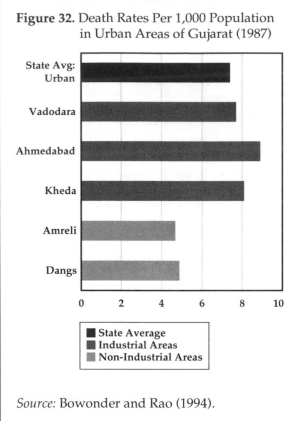

Figure 32. Death Rates Per 1,000 Population in Urban Areas of Gujarat (1987)

Source: Bowonder and Rao (1994).

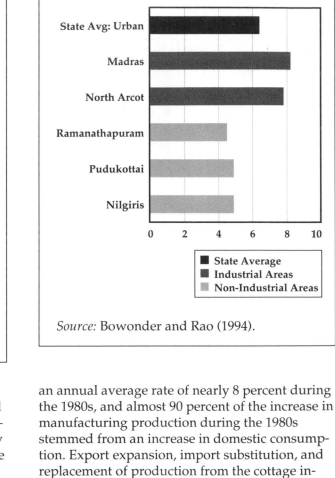

Figure 33. Death Rates Per 1,000 Population in Urban Areas of Tamil Nadu (1987)

Source: Bowonder and Rao (1994).

Over 5,600 cases were brought under the Air and Water Acts by March 1993. Of these, only 1,482—roughly one-quarter—had been decided one way or the other. Many firms find it cheaper to litigate than to comply.

D. Accelerated Growth in the 1980s

During the 1980s, industrial growth improved as industrial policy moved belatedly in the direction indicated in the *Second India Study*. As mentioned above, fiscal policy became more expansionary, stimulating consumer demand. Production in consumer goods industries—especially consumer durables—accelerated sharply. This stimulated production of industrial intermediates and capital goods. *(See Figure 34.)* The general index of industrial production increased at

an annual average rate of nearly 8 percent during the 1980s, and almost 90 percent of the increase in manufacturing production during the 1980s stemmed from an increase in domestic consumption. Export expansion, import substitution, and replacement of production from the cottage industry sector made only small contributions to the acceleration of factory output (Gupta [1993]).

Indian industry was able to respond to the increase in demand by raising production instead of enduring shortages and increasing industrial prices partly because the nation enjoyed substantial unused production capacity. Production increased far faster than the capital stock or the regular labor force grew. For reasons explained above, industry had become increasingly capital-intensive. Because of restrictive labor legislation, the factory workforce contained significant reserves. When production accelerated, underutilized equipment and workers were employed

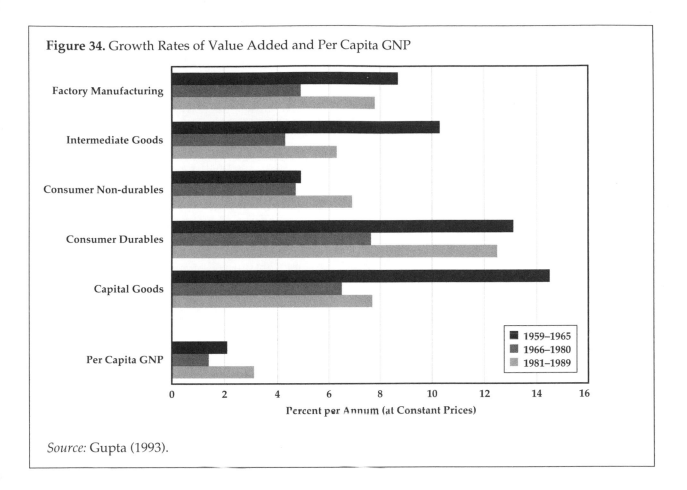

Figure 34. Growth Rates of Value Added and Per Capita GNP

Source: Gupta (1993).

more fully. Therefore, productivity increased in the use of capital, labor and materials. Capital-output ratios declined. Only in the use of energy did Indian industry become less efficient over the 1980s, largely because of low and falling real energy prices and increasing availability. Rising overall productivity allowed the prices of manufactured goods to rise less rapidly than input costs, lowering output prices in real terms. Falling real prices also stimulated the increase in demand, creating a positive feedback.

Important policy changes had positive economic effects too. Licensing requirements for new investments were relaxed in a wide range of industries. Restrictions on expansions by large Indian industrial houses were also loosened. Financial and technological collaborations with foreign firms were viewed more positively. Import licens-

ing for industrial intermediates and equipment was simplified or abandoned. Price controls and administrative rationing for many commodities were also dropped, eliminating some supply constraints. And investments in transportation and power broke important infrastructure bottlenecks.

Finally, greater competition limited how much industrialists could raise prices and profit margins as demand increased. The level of protection in most Indian industries declined substantially during the 1980s, as tariff levels were reduced and import quotas were relaxed. Declining petroleum import costs during the latter half of the 1980s and reduced needs for foodgrain imports freed up foreign exchange for industrial imports. Indian industries faced greater competition from outside. Moreover, greater flexibility for Indian producers to invest and expand implied greater domestic competition within Indian industry. These policy changes ensured a favorable supply response.

Even so, these desirable changes in industrial policy and performance did not spur more rapid growth in industrial employment. Large and medium-scale private industries, expanded with almost no increase in the regular workforce, partly because they made better use of their existing workers and partly because they increasingly resorted to using contract, casual, and temporary workers to skirt inflexible Indian labor regulations.

Moreover, the expansionary impetus of a loose fiscal policy ran into balance of payments constraints in the early 1990s. Ballooning budgetary deficits and increasing demands for imports ran into a world recession and the collapse of the Soviet economy in the early 1990s, both of which adversely affected Indian exports. A sharp demand contraction was inevitable, and reduced the industrial growth rate. Whether a more rapid rate of industrial growth can be regained without the stimulus of unsustainable fiscal deficits, and whether this can be translated into more rapid growth in industrial employment, remain to be seen.

IX. Facing the Future

Fertility rates in most of India have far to fall before they reach replacement level. The age structure is still heavily weighted with younger women, so the next generation of mothers will be much larger than this one. Consequently, huge additions to India's current population seem inevitable—possibly another doubling. What lessons do developments of the past two decades hold that might help in dealing with future population increases? Are there insights in the *Second India Study* still relevant to the Third, and possibly to a Fourth India?

In order to contain future population growth, experience shows the importance of changing *both* the social conditions that support high birth and death rates *and* the way family planning and maternal/child health services are provided in most parts of India. Poverty, isolation, social and economic disempowerment of women, illiteracy and other manifestations of underdevelopment have high costs. One is the persistence of high levels of ill health and mortality. Another is fertility that starts at very young ages and prejudices the welfare of mother and child. It is often argued that changing these deep-rooted social conditions is a long-term proposition, which must yield priority to the more feasible short-run pursuit of targeted family planning and public health interventions, but experience shows the flaw in this point of view. In parts of India where social conditions remain backward, more than three decades of targeted intervention on a massive scale have only dented the problem. In other parts of India, where rapid economic development, extensive contact with modernizing forces, or less gender-biassed social structures have supported targeted interventions, declines in birth and death rates have been rapid and the demographic transition is virtually complete. Social change can be rapid when supported by modern communications, visible political leadership, increased personal mobility, and economic and educational opportunities.

Centering maternal/child health and family planning services on clients' needs also implies a major transition. Critiques of the family planning program in the *Second India Study* and in assessments twenty years later found excessive emphasis on extending coverage to new acceptors, at the expense of sensitive continuing follow-up of existing clients; inadequate integration of family planning with reproductive and infant health services; overreliance on sterilization, especially of women, at the expense of spacing methods; overreliance on administrative targets and financial incentives at the expense of education and broader community outreach; and underuse of non-governmental and private sector service providers.

Making this transition involves no more than fully implementing the Government of India's own current population policy: it pledges to provide family planning services in the context of maternal and child health care; to offer an appropriate choice of contraceptive methods on a voluntary basis; to use multiple service providers, including NGOs, commercial channels, and private physicians; to conduct widespread community outreach, information and education programs; and to promote improvements in women's status, educational and employment opportunities. However, making these ideals a reality while simultaneously extending coverage to tens of millions of additional women will require substantial investments in training and new facilities, significant upgrading in management, and a thorough reexamination of the ways in which policy and program are implemented.

Even if these changes are made, the likely increases in population and per capita incomes imply that agricultural output must expand at least as rapidly in the coming decades as in the past. Virtually all the additional output must come through increasing yields on a constant or shrinking cropland area. The prospects seem generally less favorable today than when the *Second India Study* was written. No new technological breakthroughs comparable to the package of high-yielding, input-responsive seed varieties that sparked the Green Revolution have been demonstrated. For the main cereal crops the yield frontier doesn't seem to be expanding. Yield increases in the two decades since the *Second India Study* have been supported by ever-rising input subsidies, which have already exceeded a fiscally sustainable level. At the same time, pressures on the agricultural resource base from ecological degradation and expanding population are more pronounced. Overdrafts on groundwater, deterioration of surface irrigation systems, soil degradation through salinization, erosion, loss of nutrients and organic matter have proceeded virtually unchecked for the past two decades. In the coming decades, climate change could disrupt hydrological systems in India in unpredictable and potentially calamitous ways.

Particularly acute is the need to manage water resources efficiently and sustainably, because irrigation has driven yield increases since the 1960s. The economic potential for extending ground and surface systems or replacing those that have deteriorated is now more limited. The main challenges are institutional. Property rights to groundwater need to be clearly and enforceably defined, to prevent overdrafts, to promote efficient use, and

to ensure more equitable access of this valuable resource. Incentive mechanisms are needed to induce coordinated use of surface and groundwater flows, and to develop still underutilized groundwater resources in such states as Bihar, where farms are small, tenancy is rife, and rainfall is relatively abundant.

Institutional reforms of public sector irrigation emphasized in the *Second India Study* are still overdue. If anything, performance since then has deteriorated. Returns on invested capital and on diverted water are low. Rather than delivering high-quality irrigation services to farmers, the system mainly delivers economic rents and political benefits to contractors, bureaucrats, elected officials and local elites. The institutional challenge is formidable. Beneficiaries must be made financially responsible for irrigation investments, and irrigation managers accountable to clients. Both physical works and the operating staff need to be upgraded so that irrigation deliveries to the farm are timely, predictable and adequate. Improvements in quality must take precedence over new construction. Difficult though it has been to achieve over the past decades, India's antiquated irrigation system must be modernized if necessary yield increases are to be obtained.

Institutional reforms are no less imperative in dryland farming regions, where yields have lagged and vital woodlands and pasturelands have grossly deteriorated. Evidence shows that success must be built upon local community organization and initiative. Devolving responsibilities and resources to local government and nongovernmental organizations, as India has begun to do, acts on this principle. Programs run by central and state government agencies have a critical supportive role, providing resources, technical assistance, infrastructure, and common facilities. However, these inputs must be coordinated locally, rather than provided on a centralized, top-down pattern, so that they are appropriate and sufficiently flexible to meet local needs.

Also, the large agricultural research and extension establishment that India has built up needs to be re-invigorated. Farming system research to raise productivity and reduce risks on rainfed lands have so far produced limited results. Even adaptive and more basic varietal research on the main cereal crops shows sharply diminishing returns. Maintaining high professional research standards, increasing contacts and feedback among researchers, extension workers, and farmers and decentralizing programs to the level of the agro-climatic regions are important objectives.

India faces a further huge increase in the labor force, and there remains a massive backlog of workers in low-productivity, low-skill jobs.

The *Second India Study* emphasized—correctly, as it has turned out—that raising agricultural output was only a necessary condition for improving nutritional standards throughout the population. Raising per capita income levels sufficiently above the poverty line that households can afford more adequate diets is also critical. In the future, employment will continue to be the key to poverty eradication. India faces a further huge increase in the labor force, and there remains a massive backlog of workers in low-productivity, low-skill jobs. Stimulating faster growth in labor demand remains the highest economic priority.

For most of the period since the *Second India Study* was written, the Indian economy failed to meet this priority. Growth was slow, and other inputs were substituted for labor in agriculture and industry. At this point there seems to be consensus within India that overregulation, distorted prices, and an excessive role for government sector enterprises slowed economic growth and promoted increasing capital-intensity. Far-reaching changes in economic policies, which were initiated in the 1980s and continue in the 1990s, seem to have helped accelerate the growth rate and reduce capital-output ratios. Evidence that this has

helped stimulate employment is found in the rising trend in real wages.

However, most of the increase in employment has come, and will continue to come, in casual day labor and self-employment—in construction, petty trade, artisan and repair work, and other services. Factories, farms and offices will provide only a minor fraction of the jobs. The skills, strength, and productivity of the labor force will be as important as the overall growth of the economy in generating livelihoods. A labor force that is predominantly malnourished, unhealthy, and uneducated will be ill-equipped to find or create livelihoods for themselves. India has made a massive effort to make education and health widely available. Still, females, lower-income households, and disadvantaged communities are disproportionately left out, and the quality of services is often low. Other Asian developing countries have invested a higher proportion of their total output in human capital. Investing more in human capital through expanded programs of education and public health can pay double dividends. First, it will raise the productivity of the labor force, and help directly in reducing poverty. Second, it will accelerate the decline in birth and death rates, and ease the burden of future numbers.

Environmental and ecological problems will undoubtedly be more prominent in the coming decades, as India's economy and population expand. The *Second India Study* gave little attention to these issues, except for its concern with the fuelwood shortage. But, they are more and more inescapable. Increasing millions of citydwellers live in poverty—in substandard dwellings, in squatter settlements without adequate services, highly exposed to communicable diseases and urban or industrial pollution. Growing vehicular emissions and toxic industrial effluents compound the risks of poverty-related illness. In rural areas, populations are caught in a vicious cycle of increasing demands on ever more degraded natural systems. Experience has accumulated within India on aproaches that can successfully reverse these cycles, building on local participation. It has also been shown that industrial pollution can be controlled at costs that are low relative to the human damages that are avoided. However, the scale of India's environmental problems will require far more widespread and pervasive efforts if further degradation is to be avoided.

On completing this reassessment of population, poverty, and environmental stress in India over twenty years, one is impressed with the complexity of the linkages. Simplistic, ideologically-driven depictions of the issues seem inadequate. So do the prescriptions that are drawn from them. Many of the important challenges that the *Second India Study* foresaw for India in coping with a doubling population have indeed been major issues. India's moderate success in dealing with them generally falls within the range of *Second India Study* scenarios. But, these aggregates mask an enormous diversity of experience within India's regions and populations. Much that was unforeseen has happened, requiring new adaptations and calling for wariness in scanning the future. With a population exceeding 900 million, and hundreds of millions more inevitably to be added, India still faces a massive development challenge.

Robert Repetto is Vice President and Senior Economist at WRI and Director of the Institute's Program in Economics and Population. Formerly, he was an associate professor of economics at the School of Public Health at Harvard University and a member of the economics faculty at Harvard's Center for Population Studies.

References

Agarwal, B. (1993). "Gender, Poverty, and Environmental Change in Rural India." Institute of Economic Growth. Delhi, India. Background Paper, Second India Reassessment Study.

—. (1992). "Rural Women, Poverty and Natural Resources: Sustenance, Sustainability and Struggle for Change." In *Poverty in India—Research and Policy*. B. Harriss, S. Guhan, and R. Cassen (eds.) Delhi, India: Oxford University Press, 390–432.

Ahluwalia, I.J. (1991). *Productivity and Growth in Indian Manufacturing*. Oxford University Press: Delhi, India.

Ambannavar, J.P. (1975). *Second India Studies: Population*. MacMillan: Delhi, India.

Basu, A. (1993). "The Second India Study Revisited: The Status of Women and Demographic Change." Institute of Economic Growth. Delhi, India. Background Paper, Second India Reassessment Study.

Basu, D.N. and S.P. Kashyap (1992). "Rural Non-Agricultural Employment in India: Role of Development Process and Rural-Urban Employment Linkages." *Economic and Political Weekly* December 19: A178–A189.

Bennett, Lynn (1992). "Women, Poverty, and Productivity in India." Economic Development Institute Seminar Paper no. 43. Washington, DC: The World Bank.

Bhagwati, J.N. (1978). *Foreign Trade Regimes and Economic Development: Anatomy and Consequences of Exchange Control Regimes*. Cambridge, Mass: Ballinger.

Bhagwati and Desai (1970). *India: Planning for Industrialization and Trade Policies Since 1951*. Oxford University Press. Delhi, India.

Bhatia, P.S. (1989). "India's Family Planning Program: Emerging Issues." In *Population Transition in India*. Singh, S.N., M.K. Premi, P.S. Bhatia, & A. Bose (eds.) Delhi, India: B.R. Publishing Corporation.

Bhattacharya, Nikhilesh, et al., (1985). "Relative Price of Food and Rural Poor—The Case of India." Economic Research Unit, Indian Statistical Institute. Calcutta, India.

Bowonder, B. (1993). Background papers: *Air Pollution, Economy, Energy, Environmental Regulations, Environmental Trends, Food, Industry, Population, Resource Use, Services,* and *Water*. World Resources Institute. Washington, DC. Second India Reassessment Study.

Bowonder, B. and B. V. Rao (1994). "Environment and Industrialization in India." Administrative Staff College of India. Hyderabad, India. Background Paper, Second India Reassessment Study.

Centre for Science and Environment (1985). *The State of India's Environment: 1984–85*. The Second Citizen's Report. Delhi, India: Centre for Science and Environment.

Chambers, R. (1992). "Poverty in India: Concepts, Research and Reality." In *Poverty in India—Research and Policy*. B. Harriss, S. Guhan and R.H. Cassen (eds.). Bombay: Oxford University Press, 301–332.

___. (1988). *Managing Canal Irrigation*. Delhi, India: Oxford and IBH Publishing Co. Ltd. pp. 4, 10–45.

Chatterjee, M. (1990). "Indian Women—Their Health and Economic Productivity." World Bank Discussion Paper no. 109. Washington, DC: The World Bank.

Chaturvedi, M.C. (1976). *Second India Studies: Water*. MacMillan: Delhi, India.

Chopra, K. and S.C. Gulati (1993). "Population, Poverty and Environmental Degradation: The Role of Property Rights." Institute of Economic Growth. Delhi, India. Background Paper, Second India Reassessment Study.

Colburn, T. and C. Clement, eds. (1992). *Chemically-Induced Alterations in Sexual and Functional Development: The Wildlife/Human Connection*. Princeton Scientific Publishing Co., Inc. Princeton, NJ.

Cummings, Ralph W., Jr. (1969). "Long Range Agricultural Adjustment Analysis." unpublished. United States Agency for International Development, Delhi, India.

Dhaliwal, G.S. and V.K. Dilawari. "Impact of Green Revolution on Environment." In *Green Revolution in India*.

Ehrlich, Paul (1968). *The Population Bomb*. Ballantine Books: New York.

Ezekiel, Hannan (1975). *Second India Studies: Industry*. MacMillan: Delhi, India.

___. (1975). *Second India Studies: Overview*. MacMillan: Delhi, India.

Ezekiel, H. and M. Pavaskar (1976). *Second India Studies: Services*. MacMillan: Delhi, India.

Gadgil, M. (1990). "India's Deforestation: Patterns and Processes." *Society and Natural Resources* 3:131–143.

Gadgil, M. and V.M. Homji (1990). "Ecological Diversity." In *Conservation in Developing Countries: Problems and Prospects*. J.C. Daniels and J.S. Serrao (eds.). Proceedings of the Centenary Seminar of the Bombay Natural History Society. Bombay: Oxford University Press.

Gadgil, M. and P. Iyer (1989). "On the Diversification of Common-Property Resource Use by Indian Society." In *Common Property Resources—Ecology and Community-Based Sustainable Development*. F. Berkes (ed.). London: Belhaven Press.

Gianessi, L.P. and C.A. Puffer (1993). "Herbicide-Resistant Weeds May Threaten Wheat Production in India." *Resources* Spring:17–22. Washington, DC: Resources for the Future.

Government of India (GOI), Central Bureau of Health Intelligence (1991). *Health Information of India—1991*. Delhi, India.

___. Central Pollution Control Board (1992). *Annual Report 1991–92*. Delhi, India.

___. Ministry of Planning (1990). *Statistical Abstract: 1990*. Delhi, India.

___. Ministry of Planning (1972). *Statistical Abstract: 1972*. Delhi, India.

___. Planning Commission (1993). *Report of the Expert Group on Estimation of Proportion and Number of Poor*. Delhi, India.

___. Planning Commission (1992). *Eighth Five-Year Plan: 1992–97*. Delhi, India.

___. Registrar General (1991). *Census of India 1991*. Delhi, India.

___. Registrar General (1971). *Census of India 1971*. Delhi, India.

Gulati, A. (1989). "Input Subsidies in Indian Agriculture—A Statewise Analysis." *Economic and Political Weekly* June 24:A57–65.

Gupta, S. (1993). "Indian Manufacturing Industry: Growth Episode of the Eighties." *Economic and Political Weekly* May 29:M54–M62.

Gupta, Y.P. (1990). "Indiscriminate Use of Pesticides Poses a Serious Threat." *The Times of India*. 153 (122) II:7. Bombay, India.

Hanson, J.A. (1990) [a]. *India: Poverty, Employment and Social Services*. World Bank Country Study. Washington, DC.

—. (1990) [b]. *India: Recent Developments and Medium-Term Issues*. World Bank Country Study. Washington, DC.

Jalees, K. (1985). "Loss of Productive Soil in India." *International Journal of Environmental Studies* 24:245–250.

Jayasree, R., N. Audinarayana, G.S. Moni, and K. Mahadevan (1989). "Status of Women and Population Dynamics in Tamil Nadu." In *Women and Population Dynamics, Perspectives from Asian Countries*. Mahadevan, K. (ed.). Sage Publications. Delhi, India. pp. 320–344.

Jodha, N.S. (1992). "Common Property Resources—A Missing Dimension of Development Strategies." World Bank Discussion Papers no. 169. Washington, DC: The World Bank.

Jodha, N.S., S.M. Virmani, A.K.S. Huda, S. Gadgil, and R.P. Singh (1987). "The Effects of Climatic Variations on Agriculture in Dry Tropical Regions of India." In *The Impact of Climatic Variations on Agriculture, Vol.II*. M.L. Parry, T.R. Carter, and N.T. Konjin (Eds.) Dordrecht, The Netherlands: Reidel.

Joshi, P.K. and N.T. Singh (1991). "Environmental Issues in Relation to Incentives and Resource Allocation in Indian Agriculture." Central Soil Salinity Research Institute: Karnal, Haryana, India.

Kampen, J. and J. Burford (1988). "Production Systems, Soil-Related Constraints, and Potentials in the Semiarid Tropics, with Special Reference to India." International Crops Research Institute for the Semi-Arid Tropics. Andhra Pradesh, India.

Karkal, Malini, and Pandey et al (1989). *Studies on Women and Population—A Critique*. Himalaya Publishing House, Bombay, India.

Khandekar, R.N. (1984). "Lead Pollution from Auto Exhausts." *Science Today* 18:46–49.

Kirloskar Consultants Limited (1991). *Final Report on Environmental Profile of India*. Overseas Economic Cooperation Fund, Japan.

Krishnan, T.N. (1991). "Wages, Employment and Output in an Agrarian Economy." *Economic and Political Weekly* June 29. Vol. 26.

Kulkarni, S. (1983): "Towards a Social Forestry Policy." *Economic and Political Weekly*, Vol. 8, No. 6, Feb. 6.

Mahadevan, K. (1989). *Women and Population Dynamics: Perspectives from Asian Countries*. Sage Publications: Delhi, India.

Mathur, O.P. (1993). "The Second India Study Revisited: Urbanization, Poverty, and Environment." National Institute of Public Finance and Policy. Delhi, India. Background Paper, Second India Reassessment Study.

Mehta, F.A. (1976). *Second India Studies: Economy*. MacMillan: Delhi, India.

Mishra, A. (1986). "The Tawa Dam: An Irrigation Project That Has Reduced Farm Production." In *The Social and Environmental Effects of Large Dams*. Goldsmith, E. and N. Hildyard (eds.). Abstract. Wodebridge Ecological Centre, Cornell, Vol. III:47.

Mohan, R. (1992). "Housing and Urban Development: Policy Issues for 1990s." *Economic and Political Weekly* September 5:1913–1920.

Mundle, S. and M.G. Rao (1991). "Volume and Composition of Government Subsidies in India, 1987–88." *Economic and Political Weekly* May 4:1157–1172.

Narayana, N.S.S., K.S. Parikh, and T.N. Srinivasan (1991). *Agriculture, Growth and Redistribution of Income*. Tinbergen, J., D.W. Jorgenson, and J. Waelbroeck (eds.). Elsevier Science Publishers: B.V. Amsterdam.

National Institute of Urban Areas (1983). "A Study of Financial Resources of Urban Local Bodies in India and the Level of Services Provided." Delhi, India.

Nayar, P.K.B. (1989). "Kerala Women in Historical and Contemporary Perspective." In Mahadevan, K. (ed.). *Women and Population Dynamics: Perspectives from Asian Countries*. Delhi, India: Sage Publications.

Ninan, K.N. and H. Chandrashekar (1993). "Green Revolution, Dryland Agriculture and Sustainability—Insights from India." *Economic and Political Weekly*, 20 March: A2–A7.

Omran, Abdel R. (1971). *The Health Theme in Family Planning*. Monograph No. 16. Chapel Hill: Carolina Population Center, The University of North Carolina at Chapel Hill.

Pachauri, R.K. (1994). "Energy Scene in India—Last Two Decades." Tata Energy Research Institute. Delhi, India. Background paper, Second India Reassessment Project.

Paddock, William and Paul. (1967). *Famine—1975: America's Decision: Who Will Survive?* Little Brown: Boston.

Parikh, J. and S. Gokharn (1992). "Climate Change and India's Energy Policy Options." Indira Gandhi Institute of Development Research, Discussion Paper no. 76.

Parikh, J. and K. Parikh. "Energy Policy: Problems, Perceptions and Reforms." In *The Indian Economy*.

Parikh, K. (1993). "The Lost Decades—1971–91: What India Missed." Indira Gandhi Institute of Development Research. Bombay, India. Background Paper, Second India Reassessment Project.

—. (1976). *Second India Studies: Energy*. MacMillan: Delhi, India.

Punder, B.P. and S. Das (1985). *State of Art Report on Vehicle Emissions*. Government of India, Department of Environment, Delhi.

Radhakrishna, R. and C. Ravi (1990). "Food Demand Projections for India." Centre for Economic and Social Studies. Hyderabad, May.

Rao, V.M. (1975). *Second India Studies: Food*. MacMillan: Delhi, India.

Reddy, P.J. "Differential Status of Women and Population Dynamics in Andhra Pradesh."

Roy, S.K. (1988). "Urban Services: The Calcutta Experience." *Urban India* July/Dec. National Institute of Urban Affairs. Delhi, India.

Shah, Tushaar (1993). *Groundwater Markets and Irrigation Development—Political Economy and Practical Policy*. Bombay: Oxford University Press.

Singh, K.P. (1989). "The Status of Women in Punjab and Haryana." In *Women and Population Dynamics, Perspectives from Asian Countries*. Mahadevan, K. (ed.). Sage Publications. Delhi, India.

Sivaswamy Srikantan, K. and K. Balasubramanian (1989). "Stalling of Fertility Decline in India." In *Population Transition in India*. Singh, S.N., M.K. Premi, P.S. Bhatia, and Ashish Bose (eds.). Vol. I. B.R. Publishing Corporation: Delhi, India.

Srinivasan, K. (1993). "Demographic Transition in India since 1970—Trends and Correlates."

World Resources Institute. Washington, DC. Background Paper, Second India Reassessment Project.

Subba Rao, D.V., K.R. Chowdry and C.G. Venkata Reddy (1987). "Degradation of Agro-Ecosystem—An Explanatory Study on Cotton Farming." *Indian Journal of Agricultural Economics* 42:410–415.

Tucker, R.P. and J.F. Richards, eds. (1983). *Global Deforestation and the Nineteenth-Century World Economy*. Duke University Press. Durham, NC.

United Nations Children's Fund (UNICEF) (1991). "Children and Women in India: A Situation Analysis." Delhi, India.

United Nations Conference on Trade and Development (1993). "Trade and Environment Linkages: The Case of India". Indira Gandhi Institute of Development Research. Bombay, India. June.

Vaidyanathan, A. (1993). "Second India Series Revisited: Food and Agriculture." Madras Institute of Development Studies. Madras, India. Background Paper, Second India Reassessment Project.

—. (1993). "Second India Series Revisited: Water." Madras Institute of Development Studies. Madras, India. Background Paper, Second India Reassessment Project.

World Health Organization/United Nations Environment Programme (1992). *Urban Air Pollution in Megacities of the World*. Oxford: Basil Blackwell.

World Bank (1993). *World Development Report 1993*. Oxford: New York.

___. (1991). *Gender and Poverty in India*. World Bank Country Study. Washington, DC.

___. (1990). *India, An Industrializing Economy in Transition*. World Bank Country Study. Washington, DC.

World Resources Institute (1994). *World Resources Report 1994–95*. Oxford: New York.

World Resources Institute

The World Resources Institute (WRI) is a policy research center created in late 1982 to help governments, international organizations, and private business address a fundamental question: How can societies meet basic human needs and nurture economic growth without undermining the natural resources and environmental integrity on which life, economic vitality, and international security depend?

Two dominant concerns influence WRI's choice of projects and other activities:

The destructive effects of poor resource management on economic development and the alleviation of poverty in developing countries; and

The new generation of globally important environmental and resource problems that threaten the economic and environmental interests of the United States and other industrial countries and that have not been addressed with authority in their laws.

The Institute's current areas of policy research include tropical forests, biological diversity, sustainable agriculture, energy, climate change, atmospheric pollution, economic incentives for sustainable development, and resource and environmental information.

WRI's research is aimed at providing accurate information about global resources and population, identifying emerging issues, and developing politically and economically workable proposals.

In developing countries, WRI provides field services and technical program support for governments and non-governmental organizations trying to manage natural resources sustainably.

WRI's work is carried out by an interdisciplinary staff of scientists and experts augmented by a network of formal advisors, collaborators, and cooperating institutions in 50 countries.

WRI is funded by private foundations, United Nations and governmental agencies, corporations, and concerned individuals.

WORLD RESOURCES INSTITUTE

1709 New York Avenue, NW
Washington, DC 20006
USA